The
Power of
Reading

The
Power of
Reading

Insights from the Research

Second Edition

Stephen D. Krashen

LIBRARIES
U N L I M I T E D
A Member of the Greenwood Publishing Group

Westport, Connecticut • London

Portsmouth, NH

Library of Congress Cataloging-in-Publication Data

Krashen, Stephen D.
  The power of reading : insights from the research / by Stephen D.
  Krashen.— 2nd ed.
    p. cm.
  Includes index.
  ISBN 1-59158-169-9
  1. Books and reading. 2. Literacy. I. Title.
Z1003.K917 2004
028′.9—dc22   2004044207

British Library Cataloguing in Publication Data is available.

Library of Congress Cataloging Card Number: 2004044207
ISBN: 1–59158–169–9

First published in 2004

Libraries Unlimited, 88 Post Road West, Westport, CT 06881
A Member of the Greenwood Publishing Group, Inc.
www.lu.com

Heinemann, 361 Hanover Street, Portsmouth, NH 03801
A division of Reed Elsevier Inc.
www.Heinemann.com

Printed in the United States of America

The paper used in this book complies with the
Permanent Paper Standard issued by the National
Information Standards Organization (Z39.48-1984).

10 9 8 7 6 5 4 3

Contents

Introduction

The sophisticated skills demanded by high-level academic or professional work—the ability to understand multiple plots or complex issues, a sensitivity to tone, the expertise to know immediately what is crucial to a text and what can be skimmed—can be acquired only through years of avid reading.—Mary Leonhardt (1998)

Is There a Literacy Crisis?

I first heard about the literacy crisis in 1987 on the *Oprah Winfrey Show.* Oprah Winfrey had four adult "illiterates" as guests, people who, it was asserted, were completely unable to read and write. Their stories were touching, and by now, familiar to the reading public. They told how they had been "passed along" in school, surviving by paying careful attention in class and relying on friends. They had evolved strategies for getting through the day; for example, when they went to a restaurant with friends, they would wait to see what other people were ordering, then order the same thing.

Soon after this program, the plight of illiterates was dramatized in a made-for-TV movie starring Dennis Weaver. And soon after that, *Stanley and Iris* was released, a film telling the story of an adult illiterate. Thanks to television shows such as *Oprah Winfrey*, these films, and numerous articles in the press and in popular magazines, the public has the impression that a sizable percentage of the public is completely illiterate, that the public schools are graduating hordes of young people who can't read. The public also has the impression that illiteracy is curable by tutoring sessions that teach nonreaders to read aloud—in other words, phonics.

Both impressions are wrong. There is no literacy crisis, at least not the kind of crisis the media have portrayed. There are, first of all, very few people who have been through the educational system who are completely unable to read and write. In fact, literacy, defined simply as the ability to read and write on a basic level, has been steadily rising in the United States for the last hundred years (see, e.g., Stedman and Kaestle 1987).

There is, however, a problem. Nearly everyone in the United States can read and write. They just don't read and write well enough. Although basic literacy has been on the increase for the last century, the demands for literacy have been rising faster. Many people clearly don't read and write well enough to handle the complex literacy demands of modern society. The problem is thus not how to bring students to the second- or third-grade reading level; the problem is how to bring them beyond this.

(It is not clear, by the way, that heavy doses of phonics is the answer even at the beginning level; for extensive discussion of the most recent controversies, see Krashen 2002; Garan 2002; Coles 2003).

The cure for this kind of literacy crisis lies, in my opinion, in doing one activity, an activity that is all too often rare in the lives of many people: reading. Specifically, I am recommending a certain kind of reading—free voluntary reading (henceforth FVR). FVR means reading because you want to. For school-age children, FVR means no book report, no questions at the end of the chapter, and no looking up every vocabulary word. FVR means putting down a book you don't like and choosing another one instead. It is the kind of reading highly literate people do all the time.

I will not claim that FVR is the complete answer. Free readers are not guaranteed admission to Harvard Law School. What the research tells me is that when children or less literate adults start reading for pleasure, however, good things will happen. Their reading comprehension will improve, and they will find difficult, academic-style texts easier to read. Their writing style will improve, and they will be better able to write prose in a style that is acceptable to schools, business, and the scientific community. Their vocabulary will improve, and their spelling and control of grammar will improve.

In other words, those who do free voluntary reading have a chance. The research also tells me, however, that those who do not develop the pleasure reading habit simply don't have a chance—they will have a very difficult time reading and writing at a level high enough to deal with the demands of today's world.

FVR is also, I am convinced, the way to achieve advanced second language proficiency. It is one of the best things a second language acquirer can do to bridge the gap from the beginning level to truly advanced levels of second language proficiency.

This book examines the research on FVR, the ways FVR can be implemented, and issues related to reading, writing, and literacy. The possibilities free voluntary reading offers individuals and society are great. The goal of this book is to show the reader what free voluntary reading has to offer.

The Research

1

Free voluntary reading (henceforth FVR) means reading because you want to: no book reports, no questions at the end of the chapter. In FVR, you don't have to finish the book if you don't like it. FVR is the kind of reading most of us do obsessively all the time.

FVR is one of the most powerful tools we have in language education, and, as I argue in this chapter, FVR is the missing ingredient in first language "language arts" as well as intermediate second and foreign language instruction. It will not, by itself, produce the highest levels of competence; rather, it provides a foundation so that higher levels of proficiency may be reached. When FVR is missing, these advanced levels are extremely difficult to attain.

□ *Free voluntary reading (FVR) is the foundation of language education.*

In the following section, the evidence for the efficacy of FVR is briefly reviewed. Following this review, I argue that alternative means of promoting language and literacy development are not nearly as effective.

The Evidence for FVR

In-School Free Reading Programs

In-school free reading programs provide some of the clearest evidence for the power of reading. In these programs, part of the school day is set aside for unrestricted FVR. There are three kinds of in-school free reading programs: sustained silent reading, self-selected reading, and extensive reading. In sustained silent reading, both teachers and students engage in free reading for short periods each day (from five to 15 minutes; see Pilgreen 2000). In self-selected reading, free reading is a large part of the language arts program, with teachers holding conferences with students to discuss what was read. In extensive reading, a minimal amount of accountability is required, for example, a short summary of what was read.

□ *Types of in-school FVR: sustained silent reading, self-selected reading, extensive reading.*

Table 1.1:
Results of Reading Comprehension Tests: In-School Free Reading Compared to Traditional Approaches

Duration	Positive	No Difference	Negative
Less than 7 months	8	14	3
7 months–1 year	9	10	0
Greater than 1 year	8	2	0

Table 1.1 summarizes the impact of in-school free reading programs on tests of reading comprehension. In each case, readers were compared to students in traditional programs. These were programs that emphasized assigned reading and direct instruction in grammar, vocabulary, reading comprehension, and spelling.

Two findings clearly emerge from this table: First, in-school free reading programs are consistently effective. In 51 out of 54 comparisons (94 percent), readers do as well as or better than students who were engaged in traditional programs.

Note that a finding of "no difference" between free readers and students in traditional programs suggests that free reading is just as good as traditional instruction, which confirms that free reading results in literacy growth, an important theoretical point we return to later. As we will see later, there is also strong evidence that free reading is extremely pleasant and results in superior general knowledge. Even if free reading were equivalent to direct instruction in terms of literacy development, it should therefore be the preferred option.

Second, studies that last longer show more consistently positive results. One reason for this finding is apparent to teachers who have used free reading in their classrooms: It takes a while for students to select a book. Table 1.1 suggests that programs that last longer than a year are consistently effective.[1]

In-school free reading programs are also effective for vocabulary development, grammar test performance, writing, and oral/aural language ability (Greaney 1970; Krashen 1989).

Only a few in-school reading studies have measured gains in spelling. Of these, Pfau (1967) reported no additional gains in spelling due to supplementary free reading, but Collins (1980) and Hafiz and Tudor (1990) found that those who participated in sustained silent reading made better progress in spelling than those who were in a traditional instruction program. Elley (1991) reports a split-decision: In one group, those who did in-school free reading made better progress in spelling than traditionally taught students, but in another comparison with different students, there was no difference. In no case, however, did traditionally taught students do better.[2]

Some examples illustrate the findings of in-school free reading. Much of the research summarized in table 1.1 was performed on first language acquirers in elementary school in the United States. The results of the following studies show

□ *In 51 out of 54 comparisons, students using FVR did as well as or better on reading tests than students given traditional skill-based reading instruction.*

□ *The longer FVR is done, the more consistent the results.*

that free reading is very effective with other groups as well.

McNeil, in Fader (1976), examined the effects of a free reading program on 60 reform school boys, ages 12–17. The boys were encouraged to read newspapers, magazines, and softcover books, and the reading material was the basis for classroom discussions. After one year, the readers increased their reading comprehension scores (Scholastic Achievement Test) from 69.9 to 82.7 (a gain of 12.8), while comparisons only improved from 55.8 to 60.4 (a gain of 4.6).

□ *Reform-school boys benefited from FVR.*

Elley and Mangubhai (1983) showed that free reading has a dramatic effect on second language acquirers. In their study, fourth- and fifth-grade students of English as a foreign language were divided into three groups for their 30-minute daily English class. One group had traditional audio-lingual method instruction, a second did only free reading, while a third did "shared reading." Shared reading "is a method of sharing a good book with a class, several times, in such a way that the students are read to by the teacher, as in a bedtime story. They then talk about the book, they read it together, they act out the story, they draw parts of it and write their own caption, they rewrite the story with different characters or events" (Elley 1998, pp. 1–2). After two years, the free reading group and the shared reading group were far superior to the traditional group in tests of reading comprehension, writing, and grammar.

□ *Children studying English in Fiji benefited from FVR.*

Elley (1991) also showed that free reading had a profound effect on second language acquirers in Singapore. In three studies involving a total of approximately 3,000 children, ages six though nine, and lasting from one to three years, children who followed the "Reading and English Acquisition Program," a combination of shared book experience, language experience, and free reading ("book flood") , outperformed traditionally taught students on tests of reading comprehension, vocabulary, oral language, grammar, listening comprehension, and writing.[3]

□ *Children studying English in Singapore benefited from FVR*

Elley's more recent data (Elley 1998) come from South Africa and Sri Lanka. In all cases, children who were encouraged to read for pleasure outperformed traditionally taught students on standardized tests of reading comprehension and other measures of literacy. Table 1.2 presents the data from South Africa. In this study, EFL students who lived in print-poor environments were given access to sets of 60 high-interest books, which were placed in classrooms, with another 60 made available in sets of six identical titles. The books were used for read-alouds by the teacher, shared reading, and silent reading. Table 1.2 presents data from different provinces; in every case the readers outperformed those in comparison classes, and the gap widened with each year of reading.

Table 1.2
In-School Reading in South Africa

Reading Test Scores

Province	Grade 4		Grade 5		Grade 6	
	Read	Non-Read	Read	Non-Read	Read	Non-Read
Eastern Cape	32.5	25.6	44	32.5	58.1	39
Western Cape	36.2	30.2	40.4	34.3	53	40.4
Free State	32.3	30.1	44.3	37.1	47.2	40.5
Natal	39.5	28.3	47	32.3	63.1	35.1

Source: Elley (1998)

Beniko Mason's studies show that in-school extensive reading works very well for older students studying English as a foreign language. In Mason's first study (included in Mason and Krashen 1997), experimental students were taking a required English as a foreign language class at the college level in Japan. It was, however, a special class, consisting exclusively of students who had previously failed English (termed Sai Rishu, or retakers). Students were pre- and posttested with a cloze test, which required them to fill in missing words in an English text. For one semester, students in the experimental class read graded readers, both in class and as homework. There was some "accountability" in these classes, but it was minimal: Students had to write short synopses and keep a diary in Japanese, recording their feelings, opinions, and progress. Students in the comparison classes followed the traditional grammar and translation-based curriculum.

As presented in table 1.3, even though the extensive readers started the semester with much lower test scores in English reading, they made larger gains than the traditional group and nearly caught up with them by the end of the semester.

Table 1.3
Extensive Reading in Japan: Cloze Test Results

	Pretest mean (sd)	Post test mean (sd)
Extensive Reading	22.55 (11.54)	31.40 (11.43)
Traditional	29.70 (8.23)	33.05 (8.24)

Source: Mason and Krashen (1997)

Perhaps the most important and impressive finding of this study is the clear improvement in attitude shown by the students who did extensive reading. Many of the once reluctant students of English became eager readers. Several wrote in their diaries that they were amazed at their improvement. Their diaries also indicated that they understood the stories. Also of interest is Mason's observation that students did not progress linearly from easy to hard books. Some students read easy books after reading some more difficult texts, and then returned later to harder books.

In subsequent studies, Mason showed that extensive reading was superior to traditional instruction in programs lasting for a full academic year for both university and community college students. She also demonstrated that extensive readers improve in writing as well as reading (Mason and Krashen 1997).

Shin (2001) examined the impact of a six-week self-selected reading experience among 200 sixth graders who had to attend summer school because of low reading proficiency. About 30 percent of each group were limited English proficient. Students attended class four hours per day; during this time, approximately two hours were devoted to self-selected reading, including 25 minutes in the school library. The district invested $25 per student on popular paperbacks and magazines, with most books purchased from the *Goosebumps* series. In addition, about 45 minutes per day was devoted to reading and discussing novels such as Wilson Rawl's *Where the Red Fern Grows* and Scott O'Dell's *The Island of the Blue Dolphins*. Comparison children followed a standard language arts curriculum during the summer.

☐ Goosebumps *summer was successful.*

The readers gained approximately five months on the Altos test of reading comprehension and vocabulary over the six-week period, while comparisons declined. On the Nelson-Denny reading comprehension test, the summer readers grew well over one year. On the vocabulary section, however, the groups showed equivalent gains.

In view of the many recent moves to force less proficient readers to go to summer school to increase their reading ability, Shin's program clearly offers a more pleasant and more effective alternative to the usual diet of drills and exercises.[4]

Reported Free Voluntary Reading

People who say they read more typically read better and have a more mature writing style. As is the case with in-school free reading, this result has been confirmed in many studies (for a detailed review, see Krashen 1988). I present here only a few examples.

□ *Those who say they read more read and write better.*

Anderson, Wilson, and Fielding (1988) asked fifth graders to record their activities outside of school and reported that "among all the ways children spend their time, reading books was the best predictor of several measures of reading achievement (reading comprehension, vocabulary, and reading speed), including gains in reading comprehension between second and fifth grade" (p. 285).

Postlethwaite and Ross (1992) studied schools in 32 countries whose nine-year-olds did especially well in reading, controlling for books in the home and other background factors. Of 150 possible predictors of high reading scores, free reading came in second: Students in schools in which there was more reading of books, magazines, and comics read better. The third best predictor was the amount of reading time in class.

Kim (2003) reported similar results for summer reading for a group of children who had just completed grade five. In a careful study in which he statistically controlled for a wide variety of other factors (including gender, poverty, ethnicity, attitude/motivation, and whether the child was emotionally disturbed, learning disabled, or a speaker of English as a second language), those who read more over the summer made significantly greater gains in reading comprehension. Kim calculated that reading one book over the summer was associated with a .03 standard deviation gain in reading comprehension; thus, reading five books is associated with a .15 standard deviation gain (about 3 NCE units). If such gains are cumulative, that is, if they could be repeated each summer, the impact is very substantial, even if only a modest amount of additional reading is done.

☐ *Five extra books over the summer = 3 percentiles gain.*

Studies also show a relationship between reports of amount read and spelling performance (for first language acquisition, Stanovich and West 1989; for second language acquisition, Polak and Krashen 1988), and a positive relationship between reported free reading and writing ability in Chinese has been demonstrated by Lee and Krashen (1996, 1997) and Lee (2001).

Reported Free Reading in a Second Language

Studies in both second and foreign language confirm that those who read more do better on a wide variety of tests.

☐ *FVR and the Spanish subjunctive.*

In Stokes, Krashen, and Kartchner (1998), students of Spanish as a foreign language in the United States were tested on their knowledge of the subjunctive, a verb form that students of Spanish usually find very difficult to master. The test used probed subjects' ability to actually use the subjunctive in a real situation, not simply whether they knew the rule. In fact, only subjects who were not aware that the subjunctive was the focus of the test were included in the analysis. The only significant predictor of the ability to use the subjunctive was the amount of free voluntary reading done in Spanish; the amount of formal study of Spanish, the amount of formal study specifically aimed at the subjunctive, and how long subjects had lived in a Spanish-speaking country were not significant predictors of subjunctive competence.

□ *FVR and the English relative clause.*

Similar results for mastery of the English relative clause were reported for international students living in the United States (Lee, Krashen, and Gribbons 1996).

Several studies confirm that those who read more in their second language also write better in that language (Salyer 1987; Janopoulous 1986; Kaplan and Palhinda 1981).

□ *FVR and the TOEFL.*

The amount of free reading reported is also a very good predictor of performance on the TOEFL examination, the test of academic English that international students take that assesses their competence in listening comprehension, grammar, and writing, in addition to reading comprehension. The relationship between free reading and TOEFL scores has been demonstrated by studies done with those taking the test abroad (Gradman and Hanania 1991) as well as those living in the United States (Constantino, Lee, Cho, and Krashen 1997): Those who reported more "extracurricular reading" (Gradman and Hanania) and "free reading" and "book reading" (Constantino et al.) scored higher on the TOEFL. Of great interest is the finding that the amount of "extracurricular writing" done was not a significant predictor of TOEFL scores (Gradman and Hanania).

The relationship between reported free voluntary reading and literacy development is not large in every study, but it is remarkably consistent. Nearly every study that has examined this relationship has found a positive correlation, and it is present even when different tests, different methods of probing reading habits, and different definitions of free reading are used.

Although the results of reported free voluntary reading studies are impressive, there are some problems with this research. First, the studies rely on how much reading people say they do, which may or may not be accurate. Second, one can imagine other factors that could have been responsible for literacy development. Perhaps those who read more also did other things, such as vocabulary exercises, or perhaps those who did more drills and exercises in school did better on reading tests and also became better readers and thus read more. I think these possibilities are far-fetched, but they are possible.

□ *Other explanations for literacy development are possible but not plausible.*

One could also argue that the in-school free reading studies discussed earlier also have this problem—maybe the additional reading inspired students to do more drills and exercises. This is also unlikely, but it is possible.

The Author Recognition Test

Keith Stanovich, in a series of studies, has verified the value of a simple procedure for studying the impact of reading. In the author recognition test, subjects simply indicate whether they recog-

□ *Those who recognize more authors' names have read more and have superior literacy development.*

nize the names of authors on a list. For speakers of English as a first language, scores on the author recognition test have been shown to correlate substantially with measures of vocabulary (West and Stanovich 1991; West, Stanovich, and Mitchell 1993; Lee, Krashen, and Tse 1997), reading comprehension (Cipielewski and Stanovich 1990; Stanovich and West 1989), and spelling (Cunningham and Stanovich 1990). These results have been confirmed using other first languages as well: Significant correlations have been reported between performance on an author recognition test and writing performance in Chinese (Lee and Krashen 1996), and Korean (Kim and Krashen 1998a), and between author recognition test performance and vocabulary development in Spanish (Rodrigo, McQuillan, and Krashen 1996).

Those who report reading more also do better on the author recognition test. This is true for English speakers (Stanovich and West 1989; Allen, Cipielewski, and Stanovich 1992), Korean speakers (Kim and Krashen 1998a), Chinese speakers (Lee and Krashen 1996), and Spanish speakers (Rodrigo et al. 1996).

One study also reported a positive correlation between performance on the author recognition test and the amount of reading subjects were observed doing. West, Stanovich, and Mitchell (1993) observed airport passengers waiting for flights and classified them as either readers (those who were observed to be reading for at least 10 continuous minutes) or nonreaders. Readers did significantly better on an author recognition test as well as a short vocabulary recognition test.

Only one study thus far has examined the performance of foreign language students on the author recognition test. Kim and Krashen (1998b) reported that for high school students of English as a foreign language, performance on an English author recognition test was a good predictor of performance on an English vocabulary test. In addition, those who reported more free reading in English also tended to do better on the author recognition test.

In addition to providing confirmation of the relation between recreational reading and language development, the author recognition test and similar measures (magazine recognition test, title recognition test) promise to simplify work in this area.

Read and Test Studies

Read and test studies also provide evidence for the power of reading. In read and test studies, subjects read passages containing words whose meanings are unfamiliar to them. Readers are not alerted to the presence of these words in the text, nor are they told that a vocabulary or spelling test will be given after they read the text. Rather, readers are encouraged to read the passage for its meaning. After they finish reading the passage, they are tested to see if they have acquired some or all of the meanings of the unfamiliar words or if their spelling of these words has improved. Read and test studies thus probe "incidental" learning.

☐ *Read and test studies utilize passages with unfamiliar words in context.*

Some of the most important read and test studies were done at the University of Illinois (Nagy, Herman, and Anderson 1985; Nagy, Anderson, and Herman 1987). The Illinois researchers used elementary school students as subjects and passages from elementary school textbooks as texts. Their measures of vocabulary knowledge had an important feature: They were sensitive to whether subjects had acquired just part of the

☐ *Each time an unfamiliar word is read in context, a small increase in word knowledge typically occurs.*

13

meaning of a target word. Nagy et al. (1985) concluded from their data that when an unfamiliar word was seen in print, "a small but reliable increase of word knowledge" typically occurred (Nagy and Herman 1987, p. 26).

The Clockwork Orange Study

The Clockwork Orange study (Saragi, Nation, and Meister 1978) provides a powerful demonstration of our ability to acquire vocabulary by reading. In this study, adult readers (native speakers of English) were asked to read *A Clockwork Orange* by Anthony Burgess, a novel that contains 241 words from a slang called nadsat. Each nadsat word is repeated an average of 15 times. Few readers know these words before reading the book. The versions of *A Clockwork Orange* sold in bookstores have a dictionary in the back, so readers can look up the meanings of the nadsat words.

□ *Students who read a novel with many unique words actually acquired the meaning of many of those words from context clues alone.*

In this study, subjects were simply asked to read *A Clockwork Orange* and were told that after they finished it, they would be given a test of comprehension and literary criticism. They were not told to try to learn or remember the nadsat words. What is crucial is that they were given copies of the book without the dictionary in the back. The subjects read the book on their own time and reported finishing it in three days or less. A few days later, subjects were given a multiple-choice test covering 90 of the nadsat words.

A great deal of vocabulary acquisition took place. Scores ranged from 50 percent to 96 percent correct, with an average of 76 percent—subjects picked up at least 45 words, simply by reading a novel.

Second language read and test studies confirming that vocabulary can be acquired by reading include Pitts, White, and Krashen (1989); Day, Omura and Hiramatsu (1991); Dupuy and Krashen (1993); Horst, Cobb, and Meara (1998); and Pulido (2003). In Hermann (2003), two groups of adult ESL students were tested on unknown words contained in *Animal Farm*. One group memorized the list by rote; the second read the book. The readers were not aware they would be tested on vocabulary. When tested after one week, those who memorized the list did better, but after three weeks there was no difference between the groups. Those who did rote memorization forgot words between the two tests, but the readers actually improved their scores. [5]

It is clear that some contexts give the reader better clues to the meaning of a word than others do. Nevertheless, research indicates that most contexts are helpful; Beck, McKeown, and McCaslin (1983) found that 61 percent of the contexts they examined in basal readers were of help in acquiring new vocabulary, providing at least some clues to meanings of unfamiliar words, while 31 percent were of no help and 8 percent were "misdirective."

Despite the presence of occasionally unhelpful or misdirective contexts, readers eventually arrive at meanings of many unknown words. The few that escape readers, the few that must be looked up or that readers get completely wrong, are a tiny minority compared to the enormous number successfully acquired. [6]

☐ *Most contexts are "helpful."*

Spelling

□ *Reading improves spelling.*

Spelling read and test studies yield similar re-sults (see Krashen 1989 for a detailed review). Each time readers read a passage containing words they cannot spell, they make a small amount of progress in acquiring the correct spelling.

Nisbet's study (1941) is typical. Children ages 11 to 14 read passages containing words they could not spell correctly on a pretest. After reading the passage, the children could spell an average of about one out of 25 of these words. Nisbet found this figure unimpressive and concluded that "in-tensive reading and study of a passage . . . does lead to some learning of spelling, but this gain is not sufficient . . . to justify the neglect of specific spelling instruction" (p. 11). This may, however, be enough to make a substantial contribution to spell-ing competence if readers read enough.[7]

□ *If readers read misspelled words, their spelling declines as well as the confidence of the speller.*

The hypothesis that spelling comes from read-ing is confirmed by an experience familiar to all teachers: Our spelling gets worse when we read misspelled words. A modified read and test study, in fact, confirmed that "reading student essays may be hazardous to one's spelling accuracy" (Jacoby and Hollingshead 1990, p. 357). In this study, subjects read misspelled versions of differ-ent words. Even though they read the misspelled words only once, when given a spelling test, the subjects performed significantly worse on the words they had seen misspelled than on those they had seen spelled correctly.

Jacoby and Hollingshead (1990) point out that the effect of seeing an incorrectly spelled word just one time was not large. They noted, however, that

16

much more dramatic results were produced . . . by the second author of [the] paper. In the course of collecting the data . . . she read the incorrectly spelled words a large number of times. As a result of this extended experience with those incorrect spellings, she reports having lost confidence in her spelling accuracy. She can no longer judge spelling accuracy on the basis of a word "looking right." The word might look right because it was one of our incorrectly spelled words. (pp. 356–357)

Summary

In-school free reading studies and "out of school" self-reported free voluntary reading studies show that more reading results in better reading comprehension, writing style, vocabulary, spelling, and grammatical development. Read and test studies confirm that reading develops vocabulary and spelling. Figure 1.1 summarizes the "reading hypothesis."[8]

□ *In-school FVR results in better*

- *reading comprehension*
- *writing style*
- *vocabulary*
- *spelling*
- *grammatical development*

Figure 1.1 The Reading Hypothesis

Despite these results, it could be argued that reading is only one way to develop literacy. In the following section, we examine one rival hypothesis, the hypothesis that literacy can be developed in another way, by direct instruction.

The Alternative to Free Reading:
Direct Instruction

Direct instruction can be characterized as a combination of two processes:

1. Skill-building: Skill-building means consciously learning a rule, word meaning, or spelling and then making the rule "automatic" through output practice.

□ *Can direct (skill-based) instruction complete with FVR as the best method of improving literacy?*

2. Error correction: When errors are corrected, students are expected to adjust their conscious knowledge of the rule, word, or spelling.

There are several compelling reasons why direct instruction cannot account for the development of literacy. Each of these reasons, taken alone, is sufficient. Together, the case against instruction is overwhelming. Briefly, there are three arguments against instruction:

1. Language is too vast, too complex to be taught or learned one rule or word at a time (the complexity argument).

□ *The case against direct instruction is overwhelming.*

2. Literacy development can occur without formal instruction (competence without instruction).

3. The impact of direct instruction is typically small or nonexistent. When studies do show an effect of instruction, the effect sometimes disappears with time.

The Complexity Argument

Many scholars have noted that language is too complex to be deliberately and consciously learned one rule or item at a time. This argument has been made for the acquisition of grammar (Krashen 1982), spelling (Smith 1994a), phonics

(Smith 1994b), writing style (Smith 1994a; Krashen 1984), and vocabulary (Smith 1988; Nagy, Herman, and Anderson 1985).

Perhaps the most concrete example is vocabulary. Estimates of adult vocabulary size range from about 40,000 (Lorge and Chall 1963) to 156,000 words (Seashore and Eckerson 1940), and it has been claimed that elementary school children acquire from eight (Nagy and Herman 1987) to more than 14 (Miller 1977) words per day.

□ *Language is too complex to be learned one rule or word at a time.*

Not only are there many words to acquire, there are also subtle and complex properties of words that competent users have acquired. Quite often, the meaning of a word is not nearly adequately represented by a synonym. As Finegan (1999) points out, words that appear to have the same meaning often refer to slightly different concepts or are used in slightly different ways.[9]

□ *Language users must acquire many words with many nuances of meaning and complex grammatical properties.*

Also, when we acquire a word we acquire considerable knowledge about its grammatical properties. With verbs, for example, this includes fairly straightforward properties, for example, whether they are transitive or intransitive (we can say, "John told a joke," but not "John told.") , as well as more complex properties, for example, the fact that in the sentence "John is easy to please," the subject of "please" is "someone" and not John, but John is the subject of "please" in "John is eager to please." Professional grammarians have struggled to properly describe the generalizations underlying such differences, and they are rarely taught.

Vocabulary teaching methods typically focus on teaching simple synonyms and thus give only part of the meaning of the word and none of its social meanings or grammatical properties.

□ *Teaching vocabulary lists is not efficient. The time is better spent reading.*

Competence without Instruction

There is abundant evidence that literacy development can occur without formal instruction. Moreover, this evidence strongly suggests that reading is potent enough to do the entire job alone.

The read and test studies reviewed earlier are among the most compelling cases of literacy development without instruction. Clearly, in these cases, acquisition of vocabulary and spelling occurred without skill-building or correction.

Similarly, students in in-school free reading programs (see "In-School Free Reading Programs," above) who made gains equal to or greater than children in traditional programs have demonstrated acquisition of literacy without direct instruction.

☐ *Only a small percentage of those with large vocabularies used vocabulary books to increase their vocabularies.*

People with large vocabularies and good writing ability do not generally claim to have developed them through study. Smith and Supanich (1984) tested 456 company presidents and reported that they had significantly larger vocabulary scores than a comparison group of adults did. When asked if they had made an effort to increase their vocabulary since leaving school, 54.5 percent said they had. When asked what they did to increase their vocabulary, however, about half of the 54.5 percent mentioned reading. Only 14 percent of those who tried to increase their vocabulary (3 percent of the total group) mentioned the use of vocabulary books.

Some Case Histories

Some impressive case histories strongly suggest that reading alone is enough. Richard Wright (1966) grew up in an environment in which reading and writing was disapproved of by family members; his grandmother actually burned the books he brought home, "branding them as worldly" (Wright 1966, p. 142).

Wright became interested in reading and in hearing stories at an early age, thanks to a school-teacher (a boarder at his home) who told him stories from novels. Wright struggled to gain access to reading material. He delivered newspapers only so that he could read them and used an associate's library card to take books out of a library that was restricted to whites.

Clearly in agreement with the research reported here, Wright credits reading with providing his development as a writer: "I wanted to write and I did not even know the English language. I bought English grammars and found them dull. I felt I was getting a better sense of the language from novels than from grammars" (1966, p. 275).

□ *Author Richard Wright attributed his language development to novels, not English grammars.*

Although Richard Wright depended, to a great extent, on fiction, Malcolm X (El-Hajj Malik El-Shabbaz) credited nonfiction with his literacy development. As he describes in his autobiography, Malcolm X had early success in school. He was, in fact, president of his seventh-grade class. His life in the streets, however, "erased everything I'd ever learned in school (El-Shabazz 1964, p. 154). He describes his first attempt to write a letter to Elijah Mohammed:

> At least twenty-five times I must have written that first one-page letter to him, over and over. I was trying to make it legible and understandable. I practically couldn't read my handwriting myself; it shames even to remember it. My spelling and grammar were as bad, if not worse (p. 169).

□ *Malcolm X educated himself in prison by reading.*

The change came in prison. "Many who hear me today somewhere in person, or on television, or those who read something I've said, will think I went to school far beyond the eighth grade. This impression is due entirely to my prison studies" (p. 171).

These "prison studies" consisted largely of reading. Building his vocabulary at first the hard way, by studying the dictionary, Malcolm X became a dedicated reader: "In every free moment I had, if I was not reading in the library, I was reading on my bunk. You couldn't have gotten me out of books with a wedge" (1964, p. 173).

Like Richard Wright, Malcolm X specifically gave reading the credit: "Not long ago, an English writer telephoned me from London, asking questions. One was, 'What's your alma mater?' I told him, 'Books' " (1964, p. 179).

The following cases are interesting because they confirm that language and literacy development can occur from reading in a "heritage" or family language, and in a second language. In both cases, the acquirers themselves were unaware that they had made any progress.

Segal (1997) describes the case of L., a 17-year-old 11th-grade student in Israel. L. spoke English at home with her parents, who are from South Africa, but had serious problems in English writing, especially in spelling, vocabulary, and writing style. Segal, L.'s teacher in grade 10, tried a variety of approaches:

□ *Summer reading caused a dramatic improvement in writing.*

> Error correction proved a total failure. L. tried correcting her own mistakes, tried process writing, and tried just copying words correctly in her notebook. Nothing worked. L.'s compositions were poorly expressed and her vocabulary was weak. We conferenced together over format

and discussed ideas before writing. We made little progress. I gave L. a list of five useful words to spell each week for six weeks and tested her in an unthreatening way during recess. L. performed well in the tests in the beginning, but by the end of six weeks she reverted to misspelling the words she have previously spelt correctly.

In addition, L.'s mother got her a private tutor, but there was little improvement.

Segal also taught L. in grade 11. At the beginning of the year, she assigned an essay:

> When I came to L.'s composition I stopped still. Before me was an almost perfect essay. There were no spelling mistakes. The paragraphs were clearly marked. Her ideas were well put and she made good sense. Her vocabulary had improved. I was amazed but at the same time uneasy.

□ *Summer reading caused a dramatic improvement in writing.*

Segal discovered the reason for L.'s improvement: She had become a reader over the summer. L. told her, "I never read much before but this summer I went to the library and I started reading and I just couldn't stop." L.'s performance in grade 11 in English was consistently excellent, and her reading habit has continued.

Cohen (1997) attended an English-language medium school in her native Turkey, beginning at age 12. The first two years were devoted to intensive English study, and Cohen reports that after only two months, she started to read in English, "as many books in English as I could get hold of. I had a rich, ready made library of English books at home ... I became a member of the local British Council's library and occasionally purchased English books in bookstores. . . . By the first year of middle school I had become an avid reader of English."

Her reading, however, led to an "unpleasant incident" in middle school:

> I had a new English teacher who assigned us two compositions for homework. She returned them to me ungraded, furious. She wanted to know who had helped me write them. They were my personal work. I had not even used the dictionary. She would not believe me. She pointed at a few underlined sentences and some vocabulary and asked me how I knew them; they were well beyond the level of the class. I had not even participated much in class. I was devastated. There and then and many years later I could not explain how I knew them. I just did.

Spelling without Instruction

□ *Several studies show children can learn to spell without instruction.*

There is excellent evidence that children can learn to spell without instruction. The earliest study showing this was done by Cornman (1902), who studied the effect of dropping all spelling instruction in elementary schools for three years (spelling errors were still corrected by teachers, however). Cornman concluded that the effects of spelling instruction were "negligible" and that uninstructed students continued to improve in spelling and did just as well as students in previous years' classes and students in other schools.[10]

Cornman's results were replicated by Richards (1920), who studied 78 children in grades six, seven, and eight who went without spelling instruction for one year. Richards reported that 68 percent of these children improved more than one year in spelling, 20 percent made no change, and only 12 percent got worse. An additional replication was done by Kyte (1948), who found that "excellent spellers" who were excused from spelling instruction continued to improve.

Very young children can learn to spell without instruction. Goodman and Goodman (1982) reported that their daughter Kay learned to read and spell before she came to school, without any formal instruction at home. At age six, Kay spelled 58 percent of the words on a third-grade spelling list correctly and recognized the correct spellings of 91 percent of the words.

Several researchers have found that children can spell correctly a substantial percentage of words they have not yet studied in class (Thompson 1930; Curtiss and Dolch 1939; Hughes 1966) and that children improve each year on words they have already studied (Curtiss and Dolch 1939), which is additional evidence that spelling improves without instruction.

Haggan (1991) presented evidence suggesting that adult second language acquirers can improve their spelling without instruction. Haggan reported that fourth-year Arabic-speaking English majors at the University of Kuwait made fewer spelling errors in their writing than first-year English majors, even though little emphasis was put on "systematic, explicit teaching of spelling" (p. 59) in the curriculum.

□ *Adults acquiring English improve their spelling without instruction.*

The Effect of Instruction

The studies reviewed earlier of in-school free reading programs show that when free reading and direct (traditional) instruction are compared directly, free reading is as good or better, and in long-term studies free reading is a consistent winner. In addition, Snow, Barnes, Chandler, Goodman, and Hemphill (1991) reported no significant correlations between the amount of explicit vocabulary instruction students had and gains in reading comprehension and vocabulary over four

□ *FVR is nearly always superior to direct instruction on tests of*

- *reading*
- *vocabulary*
- *writing*
- *grammar*

years. Snow et al. also found that the exclusive use of a basal reader or workbook in reading lessons was negatively correlated with gains in reading comprehension, but that the use of a workbook for homework was positively correlated with gains in reading comprehension, a result that conflicts with other results presented in this section.

□ *Almost all studies show little improvement in spelling through direct instruction.*

Although the research on the impact of in-school free reading on spelling was not conclusive, there is, however, extensive evidence from other sources showing that spelling instruction has little effect. Rice (1897) claimed to find no correlation between the amount of time children were instructed on spelling and their spelling performance.[11]

Additional evidence that spelling instruction is not very effective comes from Brandenburg (1919), who reported no improvement in spelling accuracy among college students after their psychology papers were "persistently and clearly" marked for spelling errors in one semester.

Finally, Cook (1912) showed that students have a very hard time learning and applying spelling rules. Cook gave a total of 96 high school and college students a spelling test containing words that exemplified spelling rules the students had studied the previous semester. He found no difference in accuracy among (1) students who said they knew the rules and used the rules while spelling the test words, (2) those who knew the rules but did not use them, and (3) those who did not know the rules at all. Also, the college students did better on the test, but the high school students knew more spelling rules, confirming the lack of a relationship between knowing spelling rules and spelling accuracy.[12]

I have found only two studies in which spelling instruction had a clear effect. In Thompson (1930), instruction accounted for approximately a half-year extra growth over and above that expected without instruction. I have pointed out, however (Krashen 1989), that Thompson's students put in a huge amount of time in spelling instruction. In Hammill, Larsen, and McNutt (1977), students who had spelling instruction were clearly ahead of uninstructed children in grades three and four. This advantage, however, washed out by grades five and six. At this level there was no difference between instructed and uninstructed children in spelling accuracy as measured by a standardized spelling test. Spelling instruction, when it works, may only succeed in helping children learn to spell words that they would have learned to spell on their own anyway.[13]

□ *When spelling instruction works, it may only be helping children learn to spell words they will learn to spell on their from reading.*

Wilde (1990) estimated that each spelling word learned through direct instruction requires about 20 minutes of instructional time! Here is her logic: Spelling programs, she estimated, cover about 720 words per year and typically take up 15 minutes per day, or 45 hours per year. Children, however, have probably acquired the spellings of about 65 percent of the words before they are taught and acquire another 12 percent incidentally during the year, a total of 77 percent. Assuming the children reach 95 percent mastery of the spelling list (an optimistic assumption), this means that instruction was responsible for mastery of 18 percent of the 720 words (95 percent minus 77 percent), or 130 words. At 45 hours per year, this means each word took about 20 minutes to learn to spell.

A series of studies, dating from 1935, confirms that grammar instruction has no impact on reading and writing (see reviews by Krashen 1984 and Hillocks 1986). Probably the most thorough is the New

Zealand study (Elley, Barham, Lamb, and Wyllie 1976). High school students were divided into three groups: One group studied traditional grammar in English class, a second studied transformational grammar, and a third studied no grammar. Students were tested every year for three years. Elley et al. found no differences in reading comprehension, writing style, writing mechanics, or vocabulary among the groups, and a follow-up done one year after the project ended also showed no differences among the groups. The authors concluded that "it is difficult to escape the conclusion that English grammar, whether traditional or transformational, has virtually no influence on the language growth of typical secondary students" (pp. 17–18). The study of complex grammatical constructions does not help reading (or writing); rather, mastery of complex grammar is a result of reading.[14]

Other Benefits of Reading

The Pleasure of Reading

> Let me tell you, if you don't know it from your own experience, that reading a good book, losing yourself in the interest of words and thoughts, is for some people (me, for instance) an incredible intensity of happiness. (Asimov 2002, p. 18)

☐ *The pleasure hypothesis: If an activity promotes language acquisition, it is enjoyable. But enjoyment does not guarantee language acquisition.*

In Krashen (1994), I proposed the pleasure hypothesis: Pedagogical activities that promote language acquisition are enjoyable. Of course, just because an activity is enjoyable does not mean it is good for language acquisition; some activities may be very enjoyable but may not help at all. Enjoyment is no guarantee of effectiveness. It is, however, interesting that there is strong evidence that free voluntary reading is very enjoyable.

The evidence includes work by Csikszent-mihalyi (1991), who introduced the concept of flow. Flow is the state people reach when they are deeply but effortlessly involved in an activity. In flow, the concerns of everyday life and even the sense of self disappear—our sense of time is altered and nothing but the activity itself seems to matter. Cross-cultural studies indicate that flow is easily recognized by members of widely different cultures and groups. For example, members of Japanese motorcycle gangs experience flow when riding (Sato 1992), and rock climbers experience flow when climbing (Massimini, Csikszentmihalyi, and Della Fave 1992).

Of special interest is the finding that reading "is currently perhaps the most often mentioned flow activity in the world" (Csikszentmihalyi 1991, p. 117). This finding is consistent with reports of individual pleasure readers. A resident in Walse in Northern Italy said that when he reads "I immediately immerse myself in the reading and the problems I usually worry about disappear" (Massimini et al. 1992, p. 68). One of Nell's subjects reported, "reading removes me . . . from the . . . irritations of living . . . for the few hours a day I read 'trash' I escape the cares of those around me, as well as escaping my own cares and dissatisfactions" (Nell 1988, p. 240). W. Somerset Maugham, quoted in Nell, had similar comments: "Conversation after a time bores me, games tire me, and my own thoughts, which we are told are the unfailing resource of a sensible man, have a tendency to run dry. Then I fly to my book as the opium-smoker to his pipe" (Nell 1988, p.232).

☐ *Reading is the most frequently mentioned "flow" activity.*

A number of studies confirm that students prefer in-school free reading to traditional language arts.

Bailey (1969) asked parents of 22 children in in-school free reading programs how their children reacted to in-school free reading. In response to the question, "Does your child ever complain of reading in the classroom?" all 22 responded "no." When asked, "Does your child seem more or less interested in reading this year?" 21 said "more" and one responded that there was no difference.

Gray (1969) asked 27 children who had just completed a year of individualized reading : "If you were to choose your reading program for another year, which would you choose?" All 27 chose independent reading.

□ *Students prefer reading to traditional pedagogy.*

Greaney (1970) compared two groups of sixth graders in Dublin and found clear evidence that students prefer free reading to traditional language arts activities. While both groups had 40 minutes per day of reading class, the experimental group was allowed to choose their own reading material that they could read at their own rate. After the eight-month program, the experimental students rated their reading class as significantly more interesting than the comparison group rated their traditional class (table 1.4).

Table 1.4
Free Reading versus Traditional Language Arts

Rating	Self-selected	Traditional
very interesting	28	8
reasonably interesting	9	13
neutral-boring	3	17

Source: Greaney (1970)

Ivey and Broaddus (2001) asked 1,765 sixth graders in 23 different schools which reading activities they enjoyed most in their language arts class.

The clear winners were free reading time (63 percent) and the teacher reading aloud (62 percent) (students could check more than one item).

McQuillan (1994) examined reactions of university-level foreign language and second language students to a popular literature class that included some self-selected reading. McQuillan asked students to compare self-selected reading, assigned reading, and grammar instruction: "Based on your experience this class and other second language classes, which do you believe is the most pleasurable: assigned readings, self-selected reading, or grammar?"

Because results for both second language and foreign language students were similar, McQuillan combined them. Of the 49 students, 55 percent found assigned popular reading more pleasurable, 29 percent voted for self-selected reading, and 16 percent voted for grammar.

McQuillan noted that the preference for assigned reading may have been due to the fact that the assigned readings were "well-liked material that had been popular with previous students" (1994, p. 98); those supplied by the instructor were thus good reading as well as convenient. McQuillan also asked: "Given a choice between reading popular literature and studying grammar, which would you prefer to do?" Eighty percent (n = 39) said they would prefer reading popular literature. Additional very positive reactions to free reading from foreign language students are reported by Rodrigo (1997) and Dupuy (1997, 1998).

Nell (1988) provided interesting evidence showing why bedtime reading is so pleasant. Pleasure readers were asked to read a book of their own choice, while their heart rate, muscle activity, skin potential, and respiration rate were measured;

□ *Why bedtime reading is so pleasant.*

level of arousal while reading was compared to arousal during other activities, such as relaxing with eyes shut, listening to white noise, doing mental arithmetic, and doing visualization activities. Nell found that during reading, arousal was increased, as compared to relaxation with eyes shut, but a clear decline in arousal was recorded in the period just after reading, which for some measures reached a level below the baseline (eyes-shut) condition. In other words, bedtime reading is arousing, but then it relaxes you. Consistent with these findings are Nell's results showing that bedtime reading is popular. Of 26 pleasure readers he interviewed, 13 read in bed every night and 11 "almost every night" or "most nights" (1988, p. 250).

In a review of surveys done between 1965 and 1985, Robinson and Godbey (1997) confirm the pleasure of reading: Adult Americans consistently rated reading as enjoyable. In their 1985 survey of 2,500 adults, book and magazine reading was rated 8.3 out of 10 in enjoyment, compared to 7.5 for hobbies, 7.8 for television, and 7.2 for "conversations."

The research literature is filled with informal reports confirming that children find reading in school to be very pleasant. Johnson (1965) reported that when her sixth graders were allowed to do recreational reading "there were no discipline problems" and children would occasionally ask for more reading time when the free reading period was over. Petre (1971) reported on the effect of 35-minute "reading breaks" in public schools in Maryland: "The most unusual happening when the reading break begins is total quietness. . . . One middle school principal reports a 50 percent drop in discipline cases after the school began such a reading environment" (p. 192).

Pilgreen's high school ESL students (Pilgreen and Krashen 1993) were very positive about SSR (sustained silent reading): Of Pilgreen's subjects, 56 percent reported that they enjoyed the SSR sessions "very much," while 38 percent said they enjoyed them "some," and only 7 percent reported that they only enjoyed them a little. Similarly, Sadowski (1980) asked high school students how they liked a seven-week SSR program: "Of those responding (48%), 58% gave the program strong praise and asked for its continuation, while only .09% gave the program strong negative criticism and called for its elimination" (p. 724).

Davis and Lucas (1971) studied seventh and eighth graders who did free reading for one year, and noted: "Almost without exception, the students endorsed the concept and asked for similar classes in ensuing years . . . the center counselors received many complaints that the fifth-minute periods were not long enough. The students wanted at least one hour daily in the center" (p. 743).

Thompson (1956) found that "most of the teachers using self-selection evaluate it by saying 'I like it because my children like it. All my discipline problems are solved . . .' . One teacher asked 'How do you stop them from reading? Mine take out a book as soon as they come in from recess, and start reading again as soon as spelling and arithmetic assignments are completed' "(p. 487).

Oliver (1976) noted that SSR had "a quieting effect" on fourth, fifth, and sixth graders and that it "exerts an inhibiting pressure on potentially disruptive behavior of individuals" (p. 227). Farrell (1982) noted that junior high school students during SSR showed "a reluctance to put (books) aside when the bell rang" (p. 51).

Before ending this cheerful section, I must point out that in two cases, in-school free reading was not perceived to be pleasant. Minton (1980) studied the impact of SSR in a high school over one semester. Both students and faculty were negative about the program (only 19 percent of the students thought it was an "excellent idea") and were less likely to be reading after the SSR program; 28 percent said they were currently reading a book after the program ended, compared to 55 percent before the program began. Minton discusses several possible reasons SSR flopped. The most compelling to me was the fact that SSR was implemented at the same time every day, which was very awkward and disruptive. Some students were in physical education classes, some were in industrial arts, etc.

A second negative report comes from Herbert (1987). Students in grades seven, eight, and nine had mostly negative attitudes toward SSR. Herbert provides the questionnaire used but does not provide additional details about how SSR was done. She notes, however, that most of the students had positive attitudes about reading in general.

A review of several SSR studies by Yoon (2002) revealed that those who participated in SSR showed better attitudes as reflected by their responses on attitude questionnaires. In contrast to the testimonials presented in this section, however, results were modest and were only evident for studies of grade three and younger. Yoon included several unpublished doctoral dissertations in his review and relied on the results of formal questionnaires, which could explain the difference (see Von Sprecken and Krashen 2002 for commentary on the validity and limitations of attitude scales in reading).[15]

Reading and Cognitive Development

There is little doubt that reading influences cognitive development, but it is surprisingly difficult to find direct evidence. Ravitch and Finn (1987), in their study *What Do Our 17-Year-Olds Know?*, found that those 17-year-olds who knew more, read more: Those who lived in a print-richer environment did better overall on tests of history and literature, and there was a clear relationship between the amount of reported leisure reading and performance on the literature test. Stanovich and Cunningham (1992) confirmed that college students who read more did better on the same test of history and literature that Ravitch and Finn used, and this relationship held even when nonverbal ability factors were controlled.

□ *Those who read more, know more.*

Those who read more also do better on various measures of cultural knowledge. West and Stanovich created a cultural literacy test, a checklist of 30 names of artists, entertainers, explorers, philosophers, and scientists. Those who had more print exposure did better on this test, even when other factors, such as SAT scores (West and Stanovich 1991), age, education, exposure to television (West, Stanovich, and Mitchell 1993), and nonverbal abilities (Stanovich, West, and Harrison 1995) were controlled. Stanovich and Cunningham (1993) found similar results for a test of "practical knowledge" and a test of science and social studies. Filback and Krashen (2002), in a study of Christian adults, found that the amount of voluntary Bible reading done was a good predictor of biblical knowledge, but the amount of formal Bible study was not.

Good Thinkers Read More

Studies of "good thinkers" also give us some reason to believe that reading makes you smarter. Good thinkers, however they are defined, read a great deal and have read a great deal. Simonton (1988) concluded that "omnivorous reading in childhood and adolescence correlates positively with ultimate adult success" (p. 11). Schafer and Anastasi (1968) reported that high school students considered to be creative read more than average students, with more creative students reporting that they read over 50 books per year. Emery and Csikszentmihalyi (1982) compared 15 men of blue-collar background who became college professors with 15 men of very similar background who grew up to become blue-collar workers. The future professors lived in a much more print-rich environment and did far more reading when they were young.[16]

Reading and Writing Apprehension

Free reading has additional benefits. Lee and Krashen (1997) proposed that those who read more have less "writing apprehension" because of their superior command of the written language. They reported a modest but negative correlation between the amount of reading done and scores on a writing apprehension questionnaire for Taiwanese high school students (see also Lee 2001). The modest size of the correlation ($r = -.21$) may be because other factors affect writing apprehension, such as mastery of the composing process. It is consistent, however, with reports that those with less writing apprehension enjoy reading more (Daly and Wilson 1983).

Conclusion

In face-to-face comparisons, reading is consistently shown to be more efficient than direct instruction. Other studies confirm that direct instruction has little or no effect. The conclusion we can draw from these findings can be easily stated: Reading is a powerful means of developing reading comprehension ability, writing style, vocabulary, grammar, and spelling. In addition, evidence shows that it is pleasant, promotes cognitive development, and lowers writing apprehension.

An Interpretation

Studies showing that reading enhances literacy development lead to what should be an uncontroversial conclusion: Reading is good for you. The research, however, supports a stronger conclusion: Reading is the only way, the only way we become good readers, develop a good writing style, an adequate vocabulary, advanced grammatical competence, and the only way we become good spellers.

☐ *Reading is the only way.*

There are two reasons for suspecting that this stronger conclusion is correct. First, the major alternative to reading, direct instruction, is not of much help. Second, research and theory in other areas come to the same conclusion. Researchers in early reading development have concluded that we "learn to read by reading," that we learn to read by attempting to make sense of what we see on the page (Goodman 1982; see also Flurkey and Xu 2003; Smith 1994b). In my work in language acquisition, I have concluded that we acquire language in only one way: by understanding messages, or obtaining "comprehensible input" in a low-anxiety situation (e.g., Krashen 2003a). This is precisely what free voluntary reading is: messages we understand presented in a low-anxiety environment.

If this conclusion is true, if reading is the only way, it means we have to reconsider and reanalyze what we are doing when we attempt to teach language and develop literacy directly, with drills and exercises. All we are doing when we teach language this way is testing. Traditional language arts instruction, in other words, is merely a test, a test that privileged children, who grow up with books, pass and that less fortunate children fail.

☐ Direct instruction with drills and exercises is merely testing.

Let me make this very concrete. Every Monday, in thousands of language and language arts classes, children are given a list of 20 vocabulary words. During the week they do "skill-building" exercises: Draw a line from the word to the definition, fill-in-the-blank, write three sentences with each word. On Friday, the children are tested on the words.

If you show the list of 20 words to a child who has read, who grew up with books, he probably knows 15 or 16 of the words already. He has seen them before, in *Choose Your Own Adventure, Harry Potter*, and *Batman Returns*. If he studies, he gets an A. If he doesn't study, he gets a B.

☐ Readers pass vocabulary tests; nonreaders fail.

If you show the list of 20 words to a child who did not grow up with books, the situation is very different. He may know five or six of the words. If he studies, with a heroic effort, he might get a D+. Direct language instruction for these children may be nothing more than a test that they fail. And like victims of child abuse, they blame themselves.[17]

What do we typically do for children who did not grow up with books?: more drills and exercises, more of what does not work. The title of

Richard Allington's 1980 paper summarizes the results of his research: "Poor Readers Don't Get to Read Much in Reading Groups." Those who can read well are allowed to do more free reading. Those behind in reading have to do more worksheets, workbook pages, and exercises, a practice that can only increase the gap.

□ *Poor readers get more of what doesn't work.*

The Schoolboys of Barbiana, a group of eight teenagers who were unable to succeed in the Italian school system (Schoolboys of Barbiana 1970), understood that school is a test. Their thorough analysis of failure in Italian schools revealed an undeniable social class bias: At every level, children of the poor failed at higher rates than children of professional classes. The parents of those who fail, according to the Schoolboys, are persuaded to blame the children:

> The poorest among the parents . . . don't even suspect what is going on. . . . If things are not going so well, it must be that their child is not cut out for studying. "Even the teacher said so. A real gentleman. He asked me to sit down. He showed me the record book. And a test all covered with red marks. I guess we just weren't blessed with an intelligent boy. He will go to work in the field, like us." (p. 27)

The Schoolboys, however, placed the reason for the failure of these children elsewhere. One reason they gave is that those who are successful come to school already literate.

Teachers in intermediate schools (grades six to eight) feel they are teaching literacy, because they see improvement: "When they come into the first intermediate [grade six], they were truly illiterate. But now, all their papers are all correct." What has really happened is that the less literate students have failed and have left school:

□ *The less literate are the first to fail and drop out of school.*

Who is she talking about? Where are the boys she received in the first? The only ones left are those who could write correctly to begin with; they could probably write just as well in the third elementary. The ones who learned to write at home.

The illiterate she had in the first grade are just as illiterate now. She has simply dropped them from sight. (1970, p. 49).

The problem, the Schoolboys conclude, needs to be solved at school:

At times the temptation to get rid of them [the children of the poor] is strong. But if we lose them, school is no longer school. It is a hospital that tends to the healthy and rejects the sick. It becomes just a place to strengthen the existing differences to a point of no return. (1970, pp. 12–13)

Notes

1. The following studies were used to complete table 1.1:

Duration less than seven months:

Positive: Wolf and Mikulecky 1978; Aranha 1985; Gordon and Clark 1961; Holt and O'Tuel 1989 (grade seven), Huser 1967 (grade six); Burley, 1980; Mason and Krashen 1997 (study 1, Extensive Reading); Shin 2001.

No Difference: Sperzl 1948; Oliver 1973, 1976; Evans and Towner 1975; Collins 1980; Schon, Hopkins, and Vojir 1984 (Tempe); Sartain 1960 ("good readers" group); Summers and McClelland 1982 (three groups); Huser 1967 (grades four and five); Holt and O'Tuel 1989 (grade eight); Reutzel and Hollingsworth 1991.

Negative: Lawson 1968; Sartain 1960 ("slow readers" group); San Diego County 1965.

Duration seven months to one year:

Positive: Fader 1976; Elley 1991 (Singapore, P1 survey); Jenkins 1957; Manning and Manning 1984 (peer-interaction group); Bader, Veatch, and Eldridge 1987; Davis 1988 (medium ability readers); Mason and Krashen 1997 (four-year college student study, Extensive Reading); Mason and Krashen 1997 (two-year college student study, Extensive Reading); Lituanas, Jacobs, and Renandya 1999 (Extensive Reading).

No Difference: Manning and Manning 1984 (pure SSR); Manning and Manning 1984 (student-teacher conference group); Schon, Hopkins, and Vojir 1984 (Chandler); Schon, Hopkins, and Vojir 1985 (grades seven and eight); McDonald, Harris, and Mann 1966; Davis and Lucas 1971 (grades seven and eight); Healy 1963; Davis 1998 (high-ability readers)

Duration longer than one year:

Positive: Elley and Mangubhai 1983 (grades four and five); Elley 1991 (Singapore, sample of 512); Elley 1991 (Singapore, P3 survey); Aranow 1961; Bohnhorst and Sellars 1959; Cyrog 1962; Johnson 1965.

No Difference: Cline and Kretke 1980; Elley et al. 1976.

In Davis (1988), superior gains were made by the medium-ability group (a full extra year of progress!) but the difference between the readers and comparisons was not statistically significant for the high-ability readers. Nevertheless, the high-ability readers gained an additional 5 percentile points (five months) over the comparisons. Also, the failure of the high-ability group to show significant gains can be explained: SSR works best with less mature readers: It is doubtful that readers of this note, already excellent readers, will improve with a few minutes per day of SSR. Cline and Kretke (1980) reported no difference in gains in reading in a long-term study, but subjects were junior high school students who were reading two years above grade level and had probably already established a reading habit.

In Manning and Manning (1984), students who engaged in sustained silent reading made better gains than a comparison group, but the difference was not statistically significant. Sustained silent reading was significantly better than traditional instruction, however, when readers interacted with each other, that is, when they discussed their reading with each other and shared books.

The National Reading Panel (National Institute of Child Health and Human Development 2000) claimed that the advantage shown by readers in Burley (1980) was "small." Students in SSR were compared to students in three other conditions. For one measure, the overall F was 2.72 ($p < .05$), for the other $F = 8.74$, ($p < .01$). Burley does not report the details of the follow-up comparisons, only that the readers were significantly better. It was not possible to calculate effect sizes from the data presented. It is not clear how the National Reading Panel concluded that this difference was small, especially considering the fact that the treatment lasted only six weeks and contained only 14 hours of reading. In a response to my comment, Shanahan (2000) claims that "the problem here was not with the statistics, but with the design of the study. Each of the four treatments was offered by a different teacher, and students were not randomly assigned to the groups. It is impossible to unambiguously attribute the treatment differences to the methods." This is not accurate: Student assignment was in fact random (Burley 1980, p. 158), and the four teachers were randomly assigned to one of the four groups. In addition, the group that did SSR was superior to three different comparison groups, taught by three different teachers.

The National Reading Panel interpreted Holt and O'Tuel (1989) as showing no difference between readers and comparisons in reading comprehension. This study consisted of two samples, seventh and eighth graders. According to the text of the article, for the total sample, the readers were significantly better on tests of reading comprehension. The text also states that the difference was significant for the seventh graders but not the eighth graders. In Holt and O'Tuel's Table 2, however, the reading comprehension result for grade seven is clearly not significant. The effect size for grade seven (my calculations), based on posttest means, was a substantial .58, but for grade eight it was only .07. The NRP did not mention this discrepancy. I classified the results of this study as a split-decision.

2. Tsang (1996) reported that Hong Kong middle and high school students who participated in an after-school extensive reading program lasting 24 weeks made better gains in writing than comparison students in a math program, and also did better than students who did extra writing. Readers showed better gains in content and language use, but not in vocabulary, organization, or mechanics. Tsang notes that the failure to gain in vocabulary may be due to what was read (graded, pedagogical readers), or to the insensitivity of the writing task to detect gains in vocabulary; the topic may have demanded little new vocabulary. Tudor and Hafiz (1989) and Hafiz and Tudor (1990) also

reported no improvement for the variety of vocabulary used in writing after a sustained silent reading experience; the nature of the task and/or restrictions in what was read could explain these results as well. In addition, all of these studies were relatively short term, lasting less than one academic year.

Renandya, Rajan, and Jacobs (1999) examined the progress of 49 Vietnamese government officials who took a two-month intensive English course in Singapore. Their proficiency in English was considered "low to high intermediate" before taking the course.

Part of the course consisted of extensive reading: Students were required to read either 20 books in English or at least 800 pages. Importantly, students were encouraged to read books that they could read without too much difficulty and that were interesting, and were encouraged to read different kinds of books. After reading the books, students wrote short summaries. Teachers gave feedback on the content of the summaries, with little emphasis on writing mechanics. Questionnaire results confirmed that the students found the reading to be interesting, comprehensible, and enjoyable.

Renandya et al. reported that those students who did the most reading in the class made the best gains ($r = .386$) on a general test of English (listening, reading, grammar, and vocabulary). This predictor survived a multiple regression analysis, which means that it was a significant predictor even when other factors were considered, such as the amount of reading done in English before arriving in Singapore.

Although no control group was used in this study, the results are very suggestive. It is hard to image any other source for the gains than reading

—one could argue, for example, that those who read more were the more motivated students in general and were also those who studied their grammar and vocabulary harder. I have argued, however, that direct grammar study is not particularly effective (e.g., Krashen 2003a). Finally, it could be argued that writing summaries was responsible for the gains. Research reviewed in chapter 3, as well as Tsang's results, above, indicate however that adding writing does not add to the power of reading.

3. Elley (1991) also contains some fascinating discussion of reactions to in-school free reading. Some adults were concerned about how well those in the reading sections would do on tests. Elley's data confirm that the readers do very well on tests, better in fact than those who study grammar. My view is that they do well on tests because they can't help it: Thanks to reading, they have subconsciously absorbed or "acquired" many of the conventions of writing, and using them is automatic and involuntary. In fact, I think it is fair to say that well-read people nearly always write acceptably well and find it very difficult to write poorly. Another concern raised by some of the adults was that the children in the reading sections were "merely enjoying themselves." The attitude that acquisition of language must be painful is unfortunately widespread.

4. The National Reading Panel (NRP), supported by the U.S. government, also reviewed studies of in-school reading, and reached the startling conclusion that there is no clear evidence supporting this practice (National Institute of Child Health and Human Development 2000). They were, however, able to find only 14 comparisons, all lasting less than one academic year, between students in in-school free reading programs and

comparison children, devoting only six pages of their massive report to this topic (as compared to approximately 120 pages devoted to research on phonemic awareness and phonics).

Interestingly, in-school reading did not fare badly even in the limited analysis done by the NRP, with in-school readers doing better in four cases, and never doing worse. As discussed above, even a finding of "no difference" suggests that free reading is just as good as traditional instruction and is therefore preferable, because it is more pleasant and provides benefits other than literacy development.

I have also argued (Krashen 2001) that the NRP not only missed many studies, they also misinterpreted some of the ones they included.

5.   It has been argued that the number of words acquired in these studies is not sufficient to account for growth in vocabulary or adult vocabulary size (Horst, Cobb, and Meara 1998; Waring and Takakei 2003): It has been estimated that about one million words of reading for a fifth-grade child will result in vocabulary growth of several thousand words per year, enough to account for adult vocabulary size. One million words is an average dose of reading for middle-class children (Anderson, Wilson, and Fielding 1988) and is not difficult to attain, if interesting reading material is available. Comic books, for example, contain at least 2,000 words, while teen romances, such as the Sweet Valley High series, contain 40,000 to 50,000 words (Parrish and Atwood 1985).

Horst, Cobb, and Meara (1998) reported a gain of only five words after subjects read a 20,000-word book. Extrapolated to one million words read, this means growth of only 250 words in a year. The procedure used in this study, however, was odd: Students followed along in the text while the story was read aloud in class by the teacher in six class sessions. This was done to ensure that students covered the entire text and to prevent looking up words while reading. Horst et al. assure us that students were "absorbed by the story" (p. 211), but this method means readers can not proceed at their own pace and cannot reread and pause. In addition, subjects may have acquired words from the text not included in the test, which was especially likely in this study because a long text was used (but unlikely in Waring and Takakai, discussed below, as a controlled vocabulary graded reader was used). Finally, the measures used by Horst et al. did not grant partial credit.

Waring and Takakei (2003) reported that forgetting occurred rapidly in their read and test study: Their subjects, intermediate adult students of English as a foreign language in Japan, read a graded reader of approximately 6,000 words that contained 25 words that had been changed into substitute words (e.g., "yes" became "yoot," "beautiful" became "smorty"). The substitute words appeared from one to 18 times. The reading took about one hour. On tests given immediately after the reading, subjects got about 10 right on a multiple-choice test and five right on a translation test. But three months later, scores dropped to six correct and one correct on these tests, far too little to account for vocabulary growth. The gain reported by Waring and Takakei, one word after reading a 6,000-word book, projects to less than 200 words gained from one million words read.

The results of this study suggest that vocabulary acquisition is distributed and incremental; that is, it is best done when encounters with words are spaced or spread out over time, and it happens a little at a time.

For some kinds of memorization, it has been shown that distributed practice (spaced out over time) is far more efficient than massed (all at once) practice. Bustead (1943), a replication of Ebbinghouse's original results, is relevant here. Subjects simply read a passage (they did not attempt to memorize it) several times with different time intervals between readings. If a student read a 200-line poem many times, with readings one hour apart, Bumstead reported that it would take 24 readings to memorize the poem, a total of 229 minutes of reading. If the readings were 48 hours apart, it would take only 10 readings, or 95 minutes. If the readings were 192 hours apart, it would take only eight readings, or 77 minutes. Distributed exposure can thus triple efficiency, and, of great interest to us, it is especially powerful on delayed tests (see Willingham 2002 for a review of research). Encountering words in natural texts typically provides, of course, distributed exposure to vocabulary. Waring and Takakei's treatment lasted only one hour, an example of massed exposure: Subjects did not encounter any of the target words during the interval between the treatment and the delayed tests, because the words were artificial and do not occur in normal English. This explains the rapid forgetting. (It is likely that many of the nadsat words readers of *A Clockwork Orange* recalled would have faded in three months as well; forgetting, however, would probably not be as dramatic as in Waring and Takakei, as the book was read over a longer time, a few days, as contrasted with one hour.)

Swanborn and de Glopper (1999) found that studies using tests that give partial credit when subjects get some of the meaning of the word right show higher rates of vocabulary learning. This suggests that many words are not learned all at once when they are seen in context. Rather, word knowledge grows in "small increments." At any given time, there are words we know well, words we do not know, and words in between Twadell (1973) suggested that "we may 'know' a very large number of words with various degrees of vagueness —words which are in a twilight zone between the darkness of entire unfamiliarity and the brightness of complete familiarity" (p. 73). (See Wesche and Paribakht 1996 for another way of measuring partial familiarity with vocabulary.)

Waring and Takakai allowed partial credit on their translation test, but they report that partial credit was rarely granted. This could have been due to a reluctance of subjects to guess. Also, partial credit was given when the subject gave a word with "a similar meaning," not for a word that contained some of the semantic features of the correct answer. Waring and Takakai did not include a mechanism for partial credit on their multiple-choice test; distractors did not overlap in meaning with the correct option. As noted earlier, other researchers allowed partial credit on multiple-choice tests when the subject chose a distractor that partially overlapped in meaning with the correct answer. Measures more sensitive to partial credit would have resulted in increased scores that might have matched estimates of vocabulary growth.

Laufer (2003) claims that for adult second language students, writing activities in which students use new words in sentences and essays are more effective for vocabulary acquisition than reading words in stories. In the reading condition in her study, however, subjects were provided with or looked up the meanings of unfamiliar words; her study was thus a comparison of different ways of consciously learning words. Adding to the unnaturalness, readers were either provided with marginal glosses of the unfamiliar words or looked up the unfamiliar words in the dictionary. Laufer also presents an unusual argument against relying on reading for vocabulary growth in a second language, maintaining that the amount of reading necessary for substantial vocabulary growth cannot be provided in a classroom context because so little time is available (2003, p. 273). But this is actually an argument *for* reading, because recreational reading is one of the few activities a foreign language acquirer can engage in without a classroom and without a teacher. In fact, it doesn't even require speakers of the language, and the language student can continue reading long after the class ends. There is little hope that students will continue to engage in sentence production exercises after they finish studying the language formally.

6. Most of the contexts in Schatz and Baldwin (1986) were not helpful or "facilitative"; readers could not successfully acquire unfamiliar words from them. Passages used, however, were only three sentences long. Determining the meaning of some words may take more than three sentences. Consider this example from Schatz and Baldwin: "He takes out an envelope from a drawer, and takes paper money from it. He looks at it ruefully, and then with decision puts it into his pocket, with decision takes down his hat. Then dressed, with indecision looks out the window to the house of Mrs. Lithebe, and shakes his head" (p. 443).

From just this passage, it is very hard to arrive at the meaning of "ruefully." With wider context (several pages, or even chapters) and a deeper understanding of the character and what has happened in the story, the reader would have a much better chance. (See, for example, the discussion of the *Clockwork Orange* study in the text.)

Some experimenters have been able to improve vocabulary acquisition by rewriting texts to make contexts more "facilitative" or "considerate." Although readers in these studies are able to acquire more vocabulary from altered texts, readers still acquire an impressive amount from original, unaltered texts (Herman et al. 1987; Konopak 1988).

7. See Ormrod (1986) for results similar to Nisbet's, and a similar interpretation. Gilbert's studies (Gilbert 1934a,1934b,1935) were, to my knowledge, the first read and test studies showing that spelling knowledge can be increased by reading.

8. What about assigned reading? It is reasonable to expect that assigned reading will have a positive impact on literacy development if it is interesting and comprehensible. The research is consistent with this interpretation. Rehder (1980) reported spectacular gains for high school students in reading comprehension and vocabulary after a one-semester course in popular literature, which included required reading and a limited amount of self-selection (students were allowed to choose some of the reading from a list).

Lao and Krashen (2000) reported similar results for students of English as a foreign language. They compared progress in reading over one semester between university-level EFL students in Hong Kong who participated in a popular literature class that emphasized reading for content and enjoyment and students in a traditional academic skills class. Those in the popular literature class read six novels, five assigned and one self-selected. The popular literature group made far better gains in vocabulary and reading rate. These researchers apparently succeeded in assigning reading that was genuinely interesting for their students. (See also McQuillan 1994, discussed in the text.)

But not all assigned reading is compelling: O'Brian (1931) reported that a traditional skill-building program was superior to an extensive reading program for fifth and sixth graders. The reading, however, was assigned reading on social science topics. Sixth graders interviewed by Worthy (1998) "read the books they were assigned in school, and both had enjoyed some of them but 'hated' most" (p. 513). Two years later, as eighth graders, one boy described the assigned reading in language arts class as "boring and stupid" (p. 514). Both boys were enthusiastic readers on their own, however. Bintz (1993) described several students who were considered to be "passive and reluctant" readers by teachers but who read avidly on their own. These secret readers said they "expected assigned reading to be boring" (p. 611). One 11th grader told Bintz, "I don't remember much from books I have to read in school. I do remember almost everything from books I choose to read" (p. 610).

There is, of course, good reason to assign certain books (see "Conclusions" in chapter 3 of this book), but including self-selected reading is important because it ensures that reading is understandable and is for genuine interest.

9. Finegan provides this example: The words "vagrant" and "homeless" are synonyms. "Vagrant," however, carries a negative affective meaning, while "homeless" is neutral or even positive (p. 187).

10. For a statistical analysis of Cornman's data using modern statistical procedures, see Krashen and White (1991). We confirmed that Cornman's conclusions were basically correct: Uninstructed students did just as well as instructed students on spelling words in their own compositions. We found some effect for formal instruction in spelling on some of the tests that focused students on form (words presented in a list, out of context), that encouraged the use of conscious knowledge. This finding is consistent with current language acquisition theory (Krashen 2003a).

11. See Krashen and White (1991) for a reanalysis of these data, which confirmed Rice's claims. As in our reanalysis of Cornman (1902; see note 10, this chapter), spelling instruction had some effect on tests in which students were focused on form.

12. Cook also reported that even though the students had just studied the rules, many could not recall them. Of those who did recall the rules, the version they gave was often much simpler than the version they were recently taught: "Curiously enough, most of the collegians who cited a version of the ie/ei rule as consciously used relied upon the word 'Alice' and other mnemonic devices which gave a clue to only one or two of the 11 words (relating to the ei/ei rule) . . . . No [high school] freshman cited the rule as recently taught, but four had it almost correct . . . Three [high school] seniors gave the rule substantially as taught, but nearly all the others who cited anything gave a version of something taught in earlier years, the 'Alice' rule, etc. The rule seems more likely to stick as first learned" (1912, p. 322). (The "Alice" rule is new to me; apparently it reminds writers that "i" comes before "e" except after "c.")

13. Note that Hammill, Larsen, and McNutt's results are also strong evidence that spelling development can occur without instruction, confirming the results of earlier studies.

14. See Krashen (2003a) for evidence for the limits of direct grammar instruction in second language development.

15. Von Sprecken and Krashen (2002) reviewed studies using reading attitude surveys and concluded that contrary to popular opinion there is no decline in interest in reading as children get older. Older children and adolescents have more time pressure than younger children do, and have other interests, but interest in reading remains strong (see also Bintz 1993).

16. It appears to be the case that good thinkers, as a group, read more than the general population does. After a certain point, however, the relationship between the amount of reading done and thinking is less clear. Goertzel, Goertzel, and Goertzel (1978) studied 300 "eminent personalities of our age" (subjects of biographies published after 1963 in the Menlo Park Library) and reported that almost half of the group were "omnivorous readers" (p. 11). Simonton (1984) did a reanalysis of these data, however, and found only a .12 correlation between "achieved eminence" and amount of reading done. Van Zelst and Kerr (1951) reported a modest .26 correlation between number of professional journals read regularly and productivity (published papers and inventions) in a sample of scientists (controlled for age). They also reported that the relationship between reading and productivity resulted in a bimodal curve—some less productive scientists read a great deal. Apparently, good thinkers do read a lot, but it is possible to over-read. Wallas (1926) was aware of this, noting

that "industrious passive reading" (p. 48) may interfere with problem solving.

What appears to be the case is that wide reading is clearly helpful, but when one is reading to solve specific problems, selective reading is more efficient, that is, reading what you need to read to solve the problem you are currently working on. Brazerman (1985) provides support for this idea. Brazerman examined the reading habits of top physicists and reported that they read a great deal, visiting the library frequently to keep up with current research. They distinguished, however, between "core" and "peripheral" reading, reading carefully only what was relevant to their interests at the time.

17. Research confirms that the difference among children in vocabulary size is enormous. Smith (1941) found, in fact, that some first graders had larger vocabularies than some high school students. According to Smith, the range of basic words known to first graders was from 5,500 to 32,000, and for twelfth graders from 28,200 to 73,200. Other researchers have come up with more conservative data, but still conclude that there are huge differences among children. White, Graves, and Slater (1990) concluded that "mainstream" children know about 50 percent more words than "disadvantaged" children know (see also Graves, Brunett, and Slater 1982.

The Cure

2

If the arguments presented in the previous chapter are correct, if free voluntary reading is the only way to develop adequate levels of reading comprehension, writing style, vocabulary, grammar, and spelling, the implications are clear: One of the major goals of language education should be to encourage free reading, to make sure it happens. While we have paid lip-service to the value of reading (the shopping bag I got from the market recently proclaimed "Make reading your bag: open books = open doors), there has been only limited real effort in this direction.

□ *One of the major goals of language education should be to encourage free reading.*

Access

The most obvious step is to provide access to books. It is certainly true that "you can lead a horse to water but you cannot make him drink." But first we must make sure the water is there. And when it is, horses always eventually drink.

More Access at Home Results in More Reading

The research supports the commonsense view that when books are readily available, when the print environment is enriched, more reading is done. A print-rich environment in the home is related to how much children read; children who read more have more books in the home (Morrow 1983; Neuman 1986; Greaney and Hegarty 1987; McQuillan 1998a; Kim 2003).

Lao (2003) asked prospective teachers to retrospect about their reading habits during childhood and adolescents. All 12 who described themselves as "reluctant readers" when young said they grew up in print-poor environments. All 10 who described themselves as "enthusiastic early readers" said they grew up in print-rich environments.

Better Classroom Libraries Result in More Reading

□ *When children have access to more books at home, at school, or at the public library, they read more.*

Enriching the print environments in classrooms has been shown to result in more reading. Morrow and Weinstein (1982) reported that installing well-designed library corners in kindergarten classes that previously did not have them resulted in more use of books and other "literature activities" by children during free play time. In addition, children did more free reading when the books in the library corner were more physically accessible, when they were within the children's reach, and when teachers allowed the children to take books home from the classroom library (Morrow 1982).

Better School Libraries Result in More Reading

Enriching the print environment by means of a school library results in more reading. We have know this for a long time: Cleary (1939) reported that children in a school with no school library averaged 3.8 books read over a four-week period, while children from a school with a school library averaged exactly double that figure, 7.6 books. Moreover, children from the school with the library read "better" books; 84 percent of the books they selected were on "approved lists," compared to 63 percent of the reading done by the children with no library. Gaver (1963) reported that children who had access to school libraries did more reading than children who only had access to centralized book collections (without librarians), who in turn read more than children who only had access to classroom collections. My reanalysis of Gaver's data showed a strong correlation ($r = .72$) between the number of volumes available to the children and the amount they reported reading. In a study of libraries and reading in 41 states and the District of Columbia, McQuillan (1998a) also found that better school libraries (more books) resulted in more reading,

Students take more books out of school libraries that have more books and stay open longer (Houle and Montmarquette 1984). Each of these factors affects circulation independently: Increasing the supply of books by 20 percent, according to Houle and Montmarquette, increases the number of books taken out by about 10 percent, and increasing library hours about 20 percent increases loans by 17 percent in high school libraries and about 3.5 percent in elementary school libraries. Planned trips to the library also have an effect: McQuillan and Au (2001) reported that high school students did more reading when their teachers took them to the school library on planned library visits more often.

☐ *Larger school library collections and longer hours increase circulation, as do more organized visits to the library.*

One of Lao's (2003) "enthusiastic" readers reports that her parents were avid readers and read to her, but books were not plentiful at home. "Linda" tells us that her mother got books from other sources, such as the public library and that the school library was especially important in her life: "My school library was like a second home. I was always there and loved to read."

Access to Public Libraries
Results in More Reading

Access to public libraries also affects how much children read. Heyns (1978) reported that children who live closer to public libraries read more. Kim (2003) reported a strong relationship between the amount of reading done over the summer by fifth graders and whether students said it was easy to access book at a library.

One of Lao's reluctant readers ("Eileen," in Lao, 2003, described above) who had grown up in a print-poor environment at home ("books were scarce at home . . . practically non-existent," p. 15) became a reader thanks to the public library. In the fourth grade, she discovered Judy Blume's books, and her reading "took off from there" (p. 16). (See below for a discussion of "home run" book experiences.)

Ramos reported dramatic increases in reading thanks to one visit to a public library (Ramos and Krashen 1998). In this study, second- and third-grade children who came from print-poor environments and who attended a school with a poor school library were taken to the public library monthly, during school time but before the library was open to the public. This allowed the children to explore the library, share books, and not be constrained by the need to remain quiet. Each child was allowed to take out ten books, which suddenly produced a substantial classroom library for use during sustained silent reading time and for reading at home. Three weeks after the first visit to the library, both children and parents were surveyed. It was clear that the children enjoyed their visit; most reported reading more, that reading was easier, and that they wanted to return to the library.

Parents' responses were consistent with the children's' responses and tended to show even more enthusiasm. Table 2.1 presents the details.

Table 2.1
Reactions to Library Visit

Child survey (n = 93)	
First time visited the public library:	52%
Returned to the library since the visit:	62%
Reading more since the library visit:	75%
Feel reading is easier now:	82%

☐ *One trip to a public library greatly increased enthusiasm for reading.*

Parent survey (n=75)	
Children more interested in reading since visiting the library:	96%
Notice improvement in child's reading:	94%
Child spends more time with books:	94%
Would like the library visiting program to continue:	100%
Child has asked parent to take them to the library since the visit:	67%

Source: Ramos and Krashen (1998)

Of course, the implication of this study is not simply to use the public library. The solution must come from school. The school involved in this study was lucky to have a cooperative, well-supplied public library close to the school. Others are not so lucky.

Access to books from any of the sources mentioned above (home, school, public library) will be extremely helpful, and may be enough to guarantee the establishment of a reading habit. Unfortunately many children have access to none of them. Worthy and McKool (1996) studied 11 sixth graders who "hated to read." Nine of the 11 had little access to interesting reading material at home, in the school library, or in their classroom libraries, and none had visited the public library in the year before the interview. The two students who had access to interesting reading were the only two "who read with any degree of regularity" (p. 252). Ironically, even though all were described as reluc-

☐ *Often, those who "hate to read" simply do not have access to books.*

tant readers, all appeared to be quite enthusiastic about some kinds of reading, especially "light reading" (see discussion below).

Figure 2.1 summarizes the relationship between the print environment, free voluntary reading, and the development of literacy. Confirmation that figure 2.1 is correct comes from studies of the effect of the print environment on literacy development directly, indicated by the dotted line in figure 2.1. These studies show consistent results: The richer the print environment, that is, the more reading material available, the better the literacy development. (Research reviewed in Krashen 1985a, 1988, 1989; Snow, Barnes, Chandler, Goodman, and Hemphill 1991; and Foertch 1992 is confirmation.)

☐ *The richer the print environment, the better the literacy development.*

Figure 2.1 The Relationship of Print Environment and Free Voluntary Reading to Literacy Development

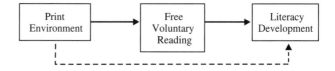

Although the relationship between the richness of the print environment and literacy development is always positive, the strength of the relationship found by researchers is often modest. One likely reason for this is that there is a missing link, or a "mediating variable": Actual free reading, as illustrated in figure 2.1. A print-rich environment will only result in more literacy development if more reading is done.

Pack (2000) provides clear evidence that simply providing access is not always enough. In a study of children's after-school activities, Pack identified a group of children he labeled "library latch-key kids," children whose parents used the public library as a "free source of after-school care" from one to six hours per day. Pack reported that the children did "little more than 'hang out' at the library" (p. 166). They did not read, but passed the entire time in socializing with other children and playing on the computer.

☐ *However, a rich print environment helps only when more reading is done.*

Providing access to books is thus a necessary, but not sufficient condition for encouraging reading. Other factors act to make free reading more desirable.

Comfort and Quiet

The physical characteristics of the reading environment are important. Morrow (1983) reported that preschool and kindergarten children used the library corner more when it had pillows, easy chairs, and carpets, and when it was partitioned off and quiet.

A particularly fascinating result was reported by Greaney and Hegarty (1987), who found that parents of fifth graders classified as heavy readers allowed their children to read in bed more than parents of fifth graders classified as nonreaders. Of the heavy readers, 72.2 percent of their parents allowed reading in bed, compared to only 44.4 percent of the nonreaders' parents.

Libraries

The first two factors for encouraging reading mentioned in this chapter, access to books and a quiet comfortable place to read, are rarely met in many students' lives, in school or outside of school. One place where these conditions can be met is the library. If many students do in fact lack access to books, and if the arguments for reading as the source of literacy development presented in chapter 1 are even partly correct, libraries are crucially important.

Children Get Their Books from Libraries

Children get a substantial percentage of their books from libraries. Table 2.2 combines data from several different studies in which 11-year-old elementary school students were asked where they got their books for free reading.

□ *Children get much of their reading material from libraries.*

There is variation in the data: In some studies, the school library is the most widely used source, in others it is the classroom library or public library. There is good agreement in all studies, however, that children get much of their reading material from some kind of library.

Table 2.2
Sources of Books for 11-Year-Old Children

Study	Percent Getting Books from Libraries
Gaver 1963	30–63
Lamme 1976	81
Ingham 1981	72–99
Swanton 1984	70
Doig and Blackmore 1995	school lib = 63; class lib = 25, public = 57
Worthy, Moorman, and Turner 1999 High SES	school = 19; class = 3; public = 14
Worthy, Moorman, and Turner 1999 Low SES	school = 34; class = 6; public = 14
Ivey and Broaddhus 2001	school = 55; class = 28, public = 61

While one study reported a decline in public library use as children get older (Williams and Boyes 1986; see esp. p. 260), the percentage of library use was still very high (86 percent of six- to seven-year-olds reported using the library, declining to 44 percent among 16- to 18-year-olds), other studies clearly show that teenagers also get many of their books from libraries (table 2.3).

Table 2.3
Sources of Books for Teenagers

Study	Age	Percent Getting Books from Libraries
Mellon 1987	ninth graders	school library—"almost 90%"; public library— girls 66%, boys 41%
Smart Girl Poll 1999	11–18	school library—66%; public library—58%
Fairbank et al. 1999	10–17	"the library"—66%; "school"—25%

Better Libraries Result in Better Reading

If libraries are a major source of books, and if more reading means better reading, better libraries should be associated with better reading. This has been found to be the case.

Gaver (1963) reported that children in schools with larger school libraries made better gains in reading than children in schools with smaller school libraries, who in turn made better gains than children in schools that had only classroom libraries.

Elley and Mangubhai (1979; reported in Elley 1984) found that the most important predictor of English reading scores among children in the Fiji Islands was the size of the school library. "Those schools with libraries of more than 400 books produced consistently higher mean scores than those with smaller libraries or none at all . . . no school had high scores without a large library" (p. 293).

□ *Library quality (books and staffing) is related to reading achievement.*

A solid confirmation of the positive effect of libraries was a remarkable study by Lance, Welborn, and Hamilton-Pennell (1993), who found that money invested in school libraries in Colorado was associated with higher reading scores, even when factors such as poverty and availability of computers were controlled. Lance and his colleagues have replicated these results in Colorado and in several others states, showing that library quality, defined in terms of the number of books in the library and the presence and quality of library staffing, is consistently related to reading achievement.[1]

The value of the library was confirmed again in Krashen (1995), an analysis of predictors of the NAEP fourth-grade reading test scores for 41 states. The results of this analysis should be of great interest to Californians, because it was California's low performance on this test relative to other states that inspired the formation of a reading task force and the perception that something was wrong with how reading was being taught in California. Among the best predictors of the NAEP performance was the number of books per student in the school library. As was the case with the Lance et al. study, this analysis controlled for other factors, such as computers and total amount of money invested in the schools. The results strongly suggest that California's real problem is access to books: California's school libraries are among the worst in the United States, both in terms of books and staffing. This suggestion was confirmed by McQuillan's work.

McQuillan (1998a) examined a wide variety of factors relating to NAEP fourth-grade reading scores in 41 states plus the District of Columbia. McQuillan also found that school libraries were a good predictor of NAEP scores. Most impressive were his findings that a very strong relationship existed between the overall print environment (school library, public library, books available in the home) and reading achievement (r = .68) and that this relationship was still substantial when the effect of poverty was considered. McQuillan also noted that California ranks very low among states in the United States not only in school libraries, but also in other sources of print, books in the home, and public libraries.

Elley (1992) surveyed reading achievement in 32 countries and found that the quality of a country's school libraries was a significant predictor of its rank in reading. Not surprisingly, Elley reported that children in more economically developed countries read much better than those in less economically developed countries. This is, most likely, because children in wealthier countries have more access to print. Of special interest to us, however, Elley also found that children in the less wealthy countries with the best school libraries made up a large percentage of the gap ("highest quarter" in table 2.4). The school library can make a profound difference.

Table 2.4
Mean Achievement by School Library Size: 14-Year-Olds

	Lowest Quarter	Second Quarter	Third Quarter	Highest Quarter
wealthy countries	521	525	536	535
less wealthy countries	445	452	454	474

mean = 500
Source: Elley (1992)

There is overwhelming evidence that children of poverty have far less access to reading material than do children from higher-income families. For these children, the school library is their only hope, the only possible source available for reading material. Sadly, the evidence thus far shows that school libraries are not succeeding in helping these children in most cases.

Poverty and Access to Books

Smith, Constantino, and Krashen (1996) investigated the availability of print in several communities in the Los Angeles area, including two vastly different ones, Beverly Hills and Watts. The difference in print environment was staggering. Children interviewed in affluent Beverly Hills said that they had an average of 200 books available to them at home (their own or siblings'). Children in low-income Watts, however, averaged less than one book, .4 to be precise. In addition, public libraries in Beverly Hills had twice as many books, and there was much more access to book stores for Beverly Hills children.

Neuman and Celano (2001) found startling differences between two high-income and two low-income print environments. Among their findings were these:

□ *Children from high-income families are "deluged" with books; children from low-income families must "aggressively and persistently seek them out."*

- There were more places to buy books in the high-income neighborhoods. Neuman and Celano looked at bookstores, drugstores, grocery stores, bargain stores, corner stores, "other" stores, and children's stores. Each low-income neighborhood had four places to buy children's books. One high-income neighborhood had 13 places, the other 11. The low-income neighborhood had no place to buy young adult books. One high-income neighborhood had three, the other one.

- High-income children had access to a much wider variety of books in stores. The total number of children's book titles available in the two low-income neighborhoods was 358 (one title for every 20 children) in one and 55 in the other (one title for every 300 children). In one high-income neighborhood, 1,597 titles were available (.3 per child), in the other, 16,455 (13 per child). Comparing the print-richest and the print-poorest, high-income children have 4,000 times the number of titles available. In low-income neighborhoods, "drugstores were the most common source of print materials for young children" (p. 15). Young adult materials were "scarce."

- Public libraries in high-income areas had far more juvenile books per child. Both libraries in the high-income neighborhood were open two evenings per week (until 8:00 P.M.); the low-income libraries were never open past 6:00 P.M.

- There was more readable environmental print in the high-income neighborhoods. Nearly all environmental signs were readable (96 and 99 percent). In the poor neighborhood, signs were often "graffiti-covered and difficult to decipher" (p. 19); only 66 and 26 percent were in "good readable condition" (p. 19).

- There were more places in public suitable for reading in the high-income neighborhood (e.g., coffee shops with good lighting, seating, friendly staff, etc.). Thus, children in the high-income communities were more likely to see people reading.

Neuman and Celano conclude that "children in middle-income neighborhoods were likely to be deluged with a wide variety of reading materials. However, children from poor neighborhoods would have to aggressively and persistently seek them out" (p. 15).

With gigantic differences such as these, it is hard to argue that children of poverty need more direct instruction in the form of phonemic awareness and phonics exercises. Our first priority is to make sure these children have something to read.[2]

Di Loreto and Tse (1999) found substantial differences in the children's section of public libraries in high-income Beverly Hills and working class Santa Fe Springs. The Beverly Hills library contained many more children's books and magazines, and had an impressive staff dedicated to children's literature, while the Santa Fe Springs library had no staff especially for the children's section (table 2.5).

Table 2.5
Comparison of Children's Section
of Public Libraries in Two Communities

	Population	Books	Children's Magazines	Staff in Children's Section
Beverly Hills	32,000	60,000	30	12
Santa Fe Springs	16,000	13,000	20	0

Source: Di Loreto and Tse (1999)

What About School?

Poverty per se is of course devastating. But schools can counter the effects of poverty in at least one area: access to books. Recall that McQuillan (1998a) found that the relationship between access to books and reading achievement held even when the effects of poverty were statistically controlled (see also Lance's studies, discussed above, as well as Roberts, Bachen, Hornby, and Hernandez-Ramos 1984, Table 3B). Thus, while it is true that children of poverty have less access to books, given two groups of such children, the group provided with more access to books will show more literacy development.

Thus far school has done little. In fact, school has not only failed to level the playing field, it has made the disparity worse.

Children from High-Income Families Go to Schools with Better Classroom Libraries

In our Beverly Hills/Watts comparison (Smith et al. 1996), we found that the classroom libraries we inspected in Beverly Hills schools averaged about 400 books; those in Watts, only about 50.

Duke (2000) reported that classroom libraries for first graders in high-income areas averaged 33 books and magazines per child, compared to 18 per child in low-income neighborhoods. During the year, an average of 19 books and magazines per child were added to the high-income libraries, but only 10 were added to classroom libraries in schools in low-income areas. Duke also noted that books in low-income classroom libraries "appeared to be older" (p. 475, n.3).

High-income area classrooms had more books on display. These classroom libraries had an average of 21 books on "full display" at the beginning of the year, with 60 more on full display over the course of the year, compared to 10 on full display at the beginning of the year in low-income classroom libraries, with an average of 16 more displayed during the year.

*Children from High-Income Families
Have Access to Better School Libraries*

Beverly Hills school libraries have two to three times as many books as those in Watts (Smith et al. 1996).

Neuman and Celano (2001) found that school libraries In high-income neighborhoods had more books per child (18.9 and 25.7, compared to 12.9 and 10) and were open more days (both were open five days per week, compared to four and two days per week for school libraries in low-income areas). Both high-income school libraries had a librarian with a master's degree. Neither low-income school library had a certified librarian. Recall that Lance and his colleagues found that the quality of library staffing was related to higher reading scores.

The disparity extends to library services. In a California study, LeMoine, Brandlin, O'Brian, and McQuillan (1997) reported that students in high-achieving schools in affluent areas are able to visit the school library more frequently, both independently and as a class, and are more likely to be allowed to take books home. Seven out of the 15 low-achieving schools they studied did not allow children to take books home.

☐ *Children who live in high-income neighborhoods go to schools with better classroom and school libraries.*

Allington, Guice, Baker, Michaelson, and Li (1995) have reported similar findings for school libraries in New York State, reporting that of the 12 school libraries they investigated, the six that served few poor children had more books than the six that served many poor children.

In agreement with Smith et al. (1996), Allington et al. also found that classroom libraries in schools serving poorer children had fewer books, and in agreement with LeMoine et al.

(1996), Allington et al. reported that "in the schools serving many poor children access to the library was usually restricted to a single weekly visit. Several schools also restricted the number of titles that children could borrow (usually one or two per visit). Two schools barred children from taking library books out of the building! No low-poverty school had such a restriction, and it was more common in these buildings for children to have relatively open access to the library throughout the day and, in some cases, before and after the regular classroom schedule" (p. 24).

The disparity extends to content as well. Children from higher-income families have access to the reading material they like, but children from lower-income families do not. Worthy, Moorman, and Turner (1999) examined access to reading for 419 sixth graders in the Austin, Texas, area. In agreement with other studies (see table 2.1), Worthy et al. found that the children were active library users: 44 percent said they usually got their reading material from some kind of library. The sample was divided into higher- and lower-income groups, based on eligibility for free and reduced lunch. The lower-income children were more dependent on libraries, especially school libraries: 63 percent of the lower-income children, for example, utilized the school library, as compared to 40 percent of the children from higher-income families.

Worthy et al. asked the children what they liked to read. The top preferences for all children, regardless of reading ability and gender, were scary books (R.L. Stine, Stephen King) and comic books (this study was done before the Harry Potter novels became popular). Worthy et al. then investigated whether these kinds of reading materials were available in three of the school libraries that served these children. The comics and magazines these children said they liked were "largely unavailable." Scary books were "moderately" available. Because of their popularity, the more recent releases were usually checked out. Nor was preferred reading available in classrooms: "While most teachers were aware of many of their students' preferences and most did not object to books like *Goosebumps* ("I'm just thrilled that they're reading'), fewer than one third of the classrooms contained more than a handful of such materials" (p. 22). Moreover, "teachers who had such materials usually used their own money to buy them or asked students to donate their used books" (p. 23). Children from higher-income families can get what they want to read outside of school; children from lower-income families often cannot and are dependent on the school and classroom libraries, which often do not include what they really want to read.

☐ *Classroom and school libraries in high-income area schools are more likely to have what children want to read.*

The tendency of some libraries to exclude what people want to read is of course not new. Michael Dirda, at age 10, noticed it: "How strange, it seemed to me, that the high-minded librarians refused to stock the Hardy Boys or Tom Corbett, the Space Cadet" (Dirda 2003, p. 59). Nell (1988) provides extensive documentation that many librarians regard themselves as "guardians of good taste."

Libraries and Second Language Acquirers

The library situation is even worse for those acquiring English as a second language. Developing literacy in the primary language is an extremely efficient means of developing literacy in the second language (Cummins 1981, Krashen 1996, 2003c). In order to become good readers in the primary language, however, children need to read in the primary language. In 1991, the average Spanish-speaking family with limited English proficient children in school in the United States had only 26 books in their home (this figure refers to total books, not age-appropriate books for children) (Ramirez, Yuen, Ramey, and Pasta 1991), about one-fifth the national average (Elley 1994). Once again, school does not solve the problem: In the bilingual schools studied by Pucci (1994), school libraries had approximately one book per child in Spanish (compare this with the national average of 18 books per child in elementary schools in the United States; Miller and Shontz 2001).

□ *Developing reading ability in the primary language helps the development of literacy in English, but there is often little to read in the primary language.*

Constantino (1994) has reported that ESL students often have little idea of what the school library can offer, and that parents of ESL students were nearly completely unaware of what was in libraries and how they operated (Constantino 1995).

Money for Libraries:
  Who Is Paying Now?

Allington et al. (1995) reported that in their survey of schools in New York State, "classrooms with the largest collections of trade books were those where teachers reported they purchased most of the books" (pp. 23–24).

A great many teachers supply their students with books from their own funds. Teachers who do this are in an impossible ethical dilemma; if they do not buy books for their students, there is nothing to read. If they do, and students progress in literacy, the basal series and unused software gets the credit. There is only one solution to this intolerable situation: a much greater investment by the school in books.

□ *A small percentage of what we spend on technology and testing would ensure access to books for all children.*

The money is there. A fraction of the investment we are willing to make for technology and testing will provide access to good reading material for all children.

A Modest Proposal

An article in the *Los Angeles Times* (MuZoz 2003) announced that first lady Laura Bush visited The Vernon City Elementary School in Los Angeles in order to award them $5,000 for the library collection. Vernon Elementary was the first school in the United States to receive money from the Laura Bush Foundation for America's Libraries. This all sounds encouraging, until we take a closer look. The article also stated that only 131 other schools in the country are getting additional funding from the Laura Bush Foundation. And 6,100 schools applied! That means only 2 percent of those that applied got funded.

There is more: The Vernon City school received enough money to add, at most, 400 titles to its library. This will raise Vernon's ratio of books per child from 15 to 1 to 16 to 1. (Recall that the national average is 18 to 1.) Also, Vernon, as a member of Los Angeles Unified School District, has no funding for a school librarian, and according to the *LA Times* article, library hours will be cut next semester because of the budget. Who is going to select the books, be responsible for their care, introduce them to children, and help teachers integrate the new books into the curriculum? When will the children have a chance to see the books?

Mrs. Bush is correct to want to help school libraries. I'm afraid, however, that the contribution of the Bush Foundation is like shooting an arrow at the moon: It is in the right direction but won't get far.

Here is another suggestion: An article in *Education Week* announced that the testing required for No Child Left Behind will cost $5.3 billion between 2002 and 2008 (Richard 2003). What if that $5.3 billion were invested instead in a trust fund for school libraries, dedicated to improving both books and staffing in high poverty area schools? The interest on this sum might be enough to guarantee a print-rich environment and adequate libraries for all children in the United States forever. (My thanks to David Loertscher for the trust fund idea.)

Another advantage of a permanent fund is that schools would no longer have to compete against each other for tiny amounts, and the time now spent writing grants, evaluating grants, and searching for money could be utilized in more productive ways.

Reading Aloud

Largely thanks to the enormous impact of Jim Trelease's *Read Aloud Handbook,* now in its fifth edition (2001), the practice of reading aloud to children is widespread in North America, and with good reason.

Children who are read to at home read more on their own (Lomax 1976; Neuman 1986, 1995). Neuman (1995) reported that parents of children who were heavy readers "established a fixed routine early on of reading to their children when they were young .. nap-time and bedtime stories were said to begin as early as six months of age" (p. 132). In addition, when teachers read stories to children and discuss the stories ("literature activities") , children read more (Morrow and Weinstein 1982). Only one of the 12 reluctant readers in Lao's study (Lao 2003; discussed earlier) was read to as a child; all 10 of the enthusiastic early readers were read to.

□ *Children who are read to at school or at home read more and show better literacy development.*

□ *Even college students read more and better books when they are read to.*

Two classroom studies confirm that children are more likely to select books for independent reading that teachers have read to them (Martinez, Roser, Worthy, Strecker, and Gough 1997; Brassell 2003).

From elementary school, the research then jumps to the college level: In Pitts (1986), "basic skills" university students ("intelligent but under-prepared students," p. 37) were read to one hour per week for 13 weeks. Selections included works by Twain, Salinger, Poe, and Thurber, and the reading was discussed afterwards. Pitts reported that the class that was read to checked out more books and better books from the reading lab than did students in other basic skills classes. In addition, the class that was read to did better on the final essay.

Reading aloud has multiple effects on literacy development. As noted above, it has an indirect effect—hearing stories and discussing stories encourages reading, which in turn promotes literacy development. Hearing stories appears to have a direct impact on literacy development as well. Short-term studies show that children make significant increases in vocabulary knowledge after just a few hearings of studies containing unfamiliar words (Eller, Pappas, and Brown 1988; Elley 1989; Leung and Pikulski 1990; Stahl, Richek and Vandevier 1991).

In controlled studies, it has been shown that children who are read to regularly, at home or at school, make superior gains in reading comprehension and vocabulary (Bus, Van Ijzendoorn, and Pellegrini 1995; Blok 1999). In a recent study by Denton and West (2002) of over 20,000 children, it was reported that children who were read to at least three times a week prior to entering kindergarten did better than those read to less than three times a week on a measure of reading, given at the end of kindergarten and the end of first grade. This result held even when the effect of poverty was controlled.

Senechal, LeFebre, Hudson, and Lawson (1996) is a remarkable confirmation that storybook reading by parents contributes to literacy development: They found that children of parents who scored higher on a test of knowledge of storybook authors and storybook titles did better on a test of vocabulary. This result held regardless of the parents' education and the parents' own reading habits.

Hearing stories read aloud is not only beneficial, it is pleasant. The empirical research confirms what most parents know: The vast majority of children say that they enjoy being read to (Walker and Kuerbitz 1979; Mason and Blanton 1971; Wells 1985; Senechal et al. 1996). Here is a concrete example. Feitelson, Kita, and Goldstein (1986) is an empirical study that confirmed the positive impact of read-alouds on language development. In addition to providing test scores, Feitelson et al. also presented this interesting report on how children reacted to hearing stories. First graders in Israel were read to from the Kofiko series, which dealt with the adventures of a monkey. The following is a quote from a teacher's observational record, two months after the reading program began: "11:20: The class is busy copying home assignment questions from the blackboard. At 11:25 the teacher reminds the children that 'we need to hurry because we want to read Kofiko.' There are immediate shouts of approval and children hurry to finish the task. A few faster children go to the desks of the slower ones and assist them. Cries of 'hurry up' and 'let's get it done so we don't lose time,' are heard from various directions" (p. 348).

□ *Nearly all children like being read to.*

In addition to the enthusiasm for hearing stories in the classroom, Feitelson et al. reported that children asked their parents to buy them Kofiko books: "By the end of the study 13 of the 31 children in the experimental class personally owned one or more Kofiko books; all together the children owned 45 Kofiko books. Four additional children were borrowing Kofiko books from relatives, neighbors, or the public library. In comparison, there were single Kofiko volumes in each of three homes in one control class, and one Kofiko book each in four homes and two in a fifth home in the second control class. In every case these belonged to older siblings and the interviewed first grader had not read them" (p. 350).

Here is another stunning example of the power of read-alouds, from the first edition of Jim Trelease's *Read Aloud Handbook* (2001):

> Assigned in mid-year to teach a sixth-grade class of remedial students, Mrs. (Ann) Hallahan shocked her new students by reading to them on her first day of class. The book was *Where the Red Fern Grows*.
>
> A hardened, street-wise, proud group (mostly boys), they were insulted when she began reading to them. "How come you're reading to us? You think we're babies or something?" they wanted to know. After explaining that she didn't think anything of the kind but only wanted to share a favorite story with them, she continued reading *Where the Red Fern Grows*. Each day she opened the class with the next portion of the story and each day she was greeted with groans. "Not again today! How come nobody else ever made us listen like that?"
>
> Mrs. Hallahan admitted to me later, "I almost lost heart." Bust she persevered, and after a few weeks (the book contained 212 pages), the

tone of the class's morning remarks began to change. "You're going to read to us today, aren't you?" Or "Don't forget the book, Mrs. Hallahan."

"I knew we had a winner," she confessed, "when on Friday, just when we were nearing the end of the book, one of the slowest boys in the class went home after school, got a library card, took out *Where the Red Fern Grows,* finished it himself, and came to school on Monday and told everyone how it ended." (p. 26)

Reading Experience

Reading itself promotes reading. A consistent finding in in-school free reading studies is that children who participate in these programs are more involved in free voluntary reading after the program ends than those in traditional programs (Pfau 1967; Pilgreen and Krashen 1993). Greaney and Clarke (1973) present a spectacular example: Sixth-grade boys who participated in an in-school free reading program for eight and one-half months not only did more leisure reading while they were in the program but also were still reading more than comparison students six years later. Tse (1996) describes the case of Joyce, an adult ESL student in the United States who did not view reading as a leisure activity and had never read a book in English before coming to the United States. After participating in an extensive reading class, her attitude toward reading "changed dramatically," and she continued to read after the end of the course, and recommended that her husband take the same class, rather than a traditional class. Shin (1998) noted an improvement in attitude toward pleasure reading among 15 ESL middle school students after one year of sustained silent reading. Before the SSR experience, only three out

□ *Reading itself promotes reading.*

of 16 (23 percent) were regular pleasure readers. This increased to 56 percent (nine out of 16) at the end of a year.

Cho and Krashen (2002) documented a clear increase in interest in reading and in promoting pleasure reading in English as a foreign language among teachers in Korea after only one two-hour exposure to interesting and comprehensible children's literature. Previously, the teachers had associated reading in English with difficult pedagogical texts that were packed with difficult vocabulary and grammar; many had never experienced reading truly interesting material in another language.

Home Run Books

> When I read Garfield books in first grade, I thought I found something better than TV.

☐ *Sometimes one positive reading experience can create a reader.*

Trelease (2001) has suggested that a single very positive reading experience, one "home run book," can create a reader. Trelease took the term "home run" book from Fadiman (1947), in reference to his earliest experience in reading, a book entitled *The Overall Boys*. "One's first book, kiss, home run, is always the best." A series of three studies has confirmed that Trelease is right. In all three studies, elementary school children were asked one question: Was there was one book or reading experience that interested you in reading? Children were also asked to name the book if they could.

It was clear from students' responses that they understood the question. While most simply reported the name of a book, some added commentary, such as

"It was the Box Car Children that started me reading, because it was a good book."

"Captain Underpants! That book turned me on, because it was funny and an adventure."

"The book that got me interested was Clue, because I didn't like to read before."

"I liked to read ever since my first book, Chicka Chicka Boom Boom."

(Von Sprecken, Kim, and Krashen 2000, p. 9)

In Von Sprecken, Kim, and Krashen (2000), 53 percent of the 124 fourth graders recalled at least one home run book. In Kim and Krashen (2000), 75 percent of 103 sixth graders from a high poverty school recalled one or more home run books. Finally, in Ujiie and Krashen (2002), 82 percent of 266 fourth and fifth graders in another low-income area school recalled one or more home run books.

In agreement with other studies of favorite books (Ivey and Broaddus 2001), the children mentioned a wide variety of books. The fourth graders in Von Sprecken et al. (2000) mentioned *Animorphs* (eight students), various "scary books" (16; but 15 of the 16 mentioned a book by R. L. Stine), Marvel Comics (three), *Charlotte's Web* (two), books by Judy Blume (two), a book from the Boxcar Children series (two), *The Lion, the Witch and the Wardrobe* (two), books by Beverly Cleary (four), and many, many others. The sixth graders in Kim and Krashen (2000) mentioned, among others, *Don't Look at the Mirror, Kristy's Great Idea, The Giver, Night in the Terror Tower, The Giving Tree, The Plague, The Outsiders, Island of the Blue Dolphin, Looking for Home, Calling All Creeps, Pigs Can Fly, The Diary of Anne Frank, Goosebumps, Matilda, Annie and the Old One,* and *Go Dogs Go.* Home run books in Ujiie and Krashen (2002) included *Fear Street, Captain Underpants, The Little Mermaid, The Stone Fox, Goosebumps,* and many others.

☐ *Children mention a wide variety of "home run" books.*

Lao's (2003) subjects also differed with respect to what caused the home run experience. For one subject, it was Judy Blume. For another, it was a magazine: Her subject "Jane" tells us: "Teachers were very structured and basal readers were used as required reading. I did not like the basal reader at all and had a hard time with reading until my mother brought me a magazine called *True Confessions.* This magazine had stories about girls who were in trouble with boyfriends, mothers or life in general. I loved this magazine and from then on, I began reading" (p. 16).

The finding that readers mentioned a wide variety of books underscores the importance of providing many different titles in school and classroom libraries and introducing children to a wide range of literature in language arts. One cannot predict what book will serve as a home run experience for a particular child.

Models

Children read more when they see other people reading, both at school and at home. Morrow (1982) found that nursery school and kindergarten use of library corners increased when teachers read during sustained silent reading sessions.

Wheldall and Entwhistle (1988) examined the reading behavior of eight- and nine-year-old children during their daily SSR time and confirmed that children were significantly more engaged in actual reading while teachers were reading than when teachers were not reading.

Morrow (1983) and Neuman (1986) reported that parents of children who do more leisure reading read more than parents of children who show less interest in books. Although these parents might do other things that promote reading, these results suggest that having a model is important.

□ *Children read more when they see other people reading.*

These studies indicate that teachers should follow McCracken and McCracken's (1978) advice and actually read for pleasure during sustained silent reading time. Although this may be difficult, given the endless paperwork teachers have to deal with, the results will make the sacrifice worthwhile.

Providing Time to Read

Simply providing time to read results in more reading. Sustained silent reading, of course, provides time for reading, and as we have seen, children who have participated in SSR programs read more on their own than those who have not, both immediately after the program ends (Pilgreen and Krashen 1993) as well as years later (Greaney and Clarke 1973). There is also strong evidence that students really use SSR time for reading.

□ *Children read more when they have time to read.*

Von Sprecken and Krashen (1998) observed sustained silent reading sessions in a middle school in the middle of the school year and reported that 90 percent of the students were reading. More reading tended to take place in those classrooms in which more books were available in the classroom library (see "Access," above) in which teachers also read while students read (see "Models," above), in which students were not required to bring their own books, and in which teachers made deliberate efforts to promote certain books. In one of the 11 classes observed, there were few books, no modeling of reading, no promotion of books, and students had to bring their own books. Nevertheless, 80 percent were observed to be reading during SSR.

Cohen (1999) unobtrusively observed 120 eighth-grade students during SSR time over a two-week period and found that 94 percent were reading during SSR. She noted that enthusiasm for sustained silent reading was not high at the beginning of the school year but increased after one to two months.

Herda and Ramos (2001) reported that 63 percent of students observed in SSR sessions in grades one through twelve were actively reading; in grades one through five, the percentages were much higher, ranging from 76 percent to 100 percent. In the upper grades, students were given the option of studying or pleasure reading, and a substantial percentage took advantage of the study option. Nevertheless, a surprising percentage were reading for pleasure, ranging from 29 percent in grade 12 to 65 percent in grade nine.

Direct Encouragement

Research is sparse in this area, but it appears that simply suggesting reading to children may have an impact on the amount of reading done. Morrow (1982) reported that when nursery school and kindergarten teachers encouraged pupils to use the library corner more, the pupils did so. Lamme (1976) found that elementary school classroom libraries were used more when teachers "encouraged their use." Greaney and Hegarty (1987) found that 73 percent of the parents of "heavy readers" in the fifth grade encouraged their children to read specific books, as compared to 44 percent of the parents of nonreaders, and Neuman

(1986) reported a strong correlation (r = .53) between "parental encouragement of reading" and the amount of time children devoted to reading.

Conversely, directing children to read may backfire if the reading material is not appropriate, that is, either not interesting or not comprehensible, or both. Greaney and Hegarty also reported that more parents of nonreaders encouraged newspaper reading (41 percent, compared to 18 percent of the parents of nonreaders). One interpretation of this result is that newspaper reading was not right for these fifth graders.

☐ *Direct encouragement to read can work if reading material is interesting and comprehensible.*

The case of Ben Carson suggests that direct encouragement to read can stimulate an interest in reading and thus lead to better literacy development. Carson, now a neurosurgeon, was a poor student in the fifth grade when his mother required him to check out two books per week from the library and insisted that he report on his reading to her at the end of each week. Carson was not enthusiastic, but he obeyed his mother. What is crucial is that Carson's mother allowed him to read whatever he wanted to.

At first, Carson chose books on animals, nature, and science, reflecting his interests. Carson reported that while he was a "horrible student in the traditionally academic subjects, I excelled in fifth grade science" (1990, p. 37). As his science reading expanded, he "became the fifth grade expert in anything of a scientific nature" (p. 37).

Carson credits reading with improving his reading comprehension and vocabulary, which affected all his academic work, reporting that he became "the best student in math when we did story problems" (p. 38). Consistent with the research, reading also improved his spelling: "I kept reading all through summer, and by the time I began sixth grade I had learned to spell a lot of words without conscious memorization" (p. 39).

The initial impetus his mother provided led to dramatic results: "As I continued to read, my spelling, vocabulary, and comprehension improved, and my classes became much more interesting. I improved so much that by the time I entered seventh grade. . . . I was at the top of the class" (p. 39). Clearly, Carson's mother provided him with just the right amount of direct encouragement; because his reading was self-selected, the intrinsic pleasure of reading soon took over, and direct instruction was no longer necessary.

The critical role of self-selection is confirmed in this report from a reader interviewed by Carlsen and Sherrill (1988):

> As soon as I was progressing through the primary grades I remember a distinct lack of enthusiasm for reading because my mother tried to force books on me, which I disliked, either because they were too difficult or they were about subject matter in which I had no interest. My older sister had been extremely fond of horse stories and I could not tolerate them. (p. 138)

Of course, encouragement only works if readers have access to truly compelling books and are capable of reading them.

Shin (2003) presents another case in which direct encouragement worked: Tanesha was a sixth grader who read at the fourth-grade level and had little confidence in her reading ability. Tanesha was enrolled in a special summer program that emphasized free reading (Shin 2001). Shin observed that Tanesha could read and understand *Goosebumps,* and encouraged her to try to finish one *Goosebumps* book and read another over the weekend. Tanesha was extremely doubtful that she could do it, but surprised herself by finishing both volumes. Shin then challenged her to read a *Goosebumps* book in a single day. Despite her reluctance, Tanesha accepted the challenge and succeeded, went on to read one Goosebumps book per day for the next few weeks, and eventually moved on to *Fear Street*, and Judy Blume, reading a total of 40 books over the summer.

The conditions were right for direct encouragement to work with Tanesha. As was the case with Ben Carson, there was access to plenty of books, the reading material was compelling, and Tanesha was capable of doing the reading: She only lacked confidence.

□ *Ben Carson and Tanesha received just the right amount of direct encouragement.*

Another form of direct encouragement is informing students about the theory and research underlying free voluntary reading. This is especially important with older students, who, based on previous classes, have assumed the correctness of skill-building and direct teaching of language. Lee (1998) is a report of one successful attempt to share theory and research with students of English as a foreign language in Taiwan.

Other Factors

Other factors that appear to affect how much children read include:

Discussion and literature circles: As noted in chapter 1, Manning and Manning (1984) reported greater gains with SSR when students discussed their reading with each other in pairs and small groups. Of great interest is their finding that a group that had brief weekly individual teacher- student conferences in which "the book the student was reading was discussed and plans for further reading were set" did not make as much progress.

The "shared book experience" group in Elley and Mangubhai (1983), also discussed in chapter 1, did better than the "pure SSR" group in the first year of their study, but there were no differences after a second year. Recall that in "shared book experience," books are read to the class, discussed, read together, and acted out.

These studies focus on gains in reading achievement, not amount read, but the results are suggestive.

Peer pressure: Appleby and Conner (1965), in their description of a one-semester free reading elective high school English course, informally observed that what students read was heavily influenced by what their peers were reading. Some students, in fact, felt compelled to read what their friends were reading and ignored their own interests. Wendelin and Zinck (1983) asked fifth graders why they selected the books they did. Sixty-nine percent responded that they relied more on friends' recommendations than on teachers' recommendations. Worthy (1998), in a study of two sixth graders, concludes that peer recommendations "may be the most important motivator for voluntary reading."

☐ *Young people's reading choices are influenced by their peers.*

Book display: Morrow (1982) reported that good kindergarten and nursery school teachers know what book store owners know: When library corners have "attracting features," posters, bulletin boards, and displays related to children's literature, children show more interest in books.

Paperbacks: Lowrey and Grafft (1965) compared two groups of fourth graders, one reading hardcover books and the other reading paperback versions of the same books (the books were "known to be popular with students and teachers"). The paperback group showed a dramatic improvement in attitude toward books and reading, while the hardcover group showed no significant change. Other studies showing that children prefer paperbacks include Ross (1978), Wendelin and Zinck (1983), and Campbell, Griswald, and Smith (1988). Also, the successful Hooked on Books experiment (Fader 1976) emphasized paperbacks.

□ *Children prefer paperback books to hardcover books.*

Jim Trelease has some interesting suggestions on how parents can encourage reading. In an interview (Carter 1988), Trelease recommended "the three B's":

Book ownership: "Again and again, I meet people who tell me that name of a special book they owned and didn't have to share."

□ *Trelease's three Bs:*
* *book ownership*
* *book racks*
* *bed lamps*

Book rack: Trelease suggests keeping reading materials in book racks in the bathroom

Bed lamp: "Even at age 3, you can say to the child: You are old enough to read in bed like Mom and Dad."

In addition, teachers have used booktalks (see, e.g., Duggins 1976) and authors' visits (e.g., Reed 1985) to encourage reading.

Light Reading: Comic Books

On a November day in 1957 I found myself standing in front of Miss Grosier's first grade class in Hillcrest Elementary School, trying to think of a really good word. She had us playing this game in which each kid had to offer up a word to the class, and for every classmate would couldn't spell your word, you got a point—provided of course that you could spell the word. Whoever got the most points received the coveted gold star.

"Bouillabaisse," I said, finally.

"You don't even know what that is," Miss Grosier scolded.

"It's fish soup."

"You can't spell that."

"Can too."

"Come here. Write it," She demanded.

I wrote it. She looked it up, and admitted that it was, indeed, correct.

Easiest gold star I ever won. And right here, right now, I'd like to thank, albeit somewhat belatedly, whoever wrote the Donald Duck comic book in which I found the word bouillabaisse. Also, I'd like to thank my mother who read me that comic book and so many others when I was four and five. . . . I learned to read from those sessions long before I started school. While most of my classmates were struggling with *See Spot Run*, I was reading *Superman*. I knew what indestructible meant, could spell it, and would have cold-bloodedly used it to win another gold star if I hadn't been banned from competition after bouillabaisse. (Shooter 1986, p. A85)

☐ *The power of comic book reading: the Jim Shooter story.*

The author of this wonderful story is Jim Shooter, former editor-in-chief of the Marvel Comic Book Company. It appeared in the 1986 edition of the *Overstreet Comic Book Price Guide*.

☐ *Light reading is the way nearly all of us learned to read.*

Perhaps the most powerful way of encouraging children to read is to expose them to light reading, a kind of reading that schools pretend does not exist, and a kind of reading that many children, for economic or ideological reasons, are deprived of. I suspect that light reading is the way nearly all of us learned to read.

In this section, I focus on comic books. Comics have been very popular, and there has been some interesting research on comic book reading.

Before showing how comics can encourage reading, I present a brief history of comic books in the United States, as well as research that focuses on questions that have been of concern to the public: Are comic books "challenging" enough? Does comic book reading cause any harm? Finally, I bring the discussion around to the original concern: Can comic book reading lead to additional free voluntary reading?

A Brief History

Comics enjoyed a "Golden Age" from about 1937 to 1955, a time that saw the introduction of such characters as Superman (1938), Batman (1939), Wonder Woman (1941), and Archie (1941). During this time, 90 percent of all elementary school children and 50–80 percent of junior high school students were comic book readers (Slover 1959; Witty and Sizemore 1954; Blakely 1958. Lyness (1952) reported more modest readership of comics, but the number of children reading comics is still substantial in his study, with 69 percent of fifth-grade boys reporting reading at least four comics a week and 46 percent reading 10 or more.

☐ *The golden age of comic books.*

Public concern about the impact of comic books on behavior, stimulated in part by Wertham's *Seduction of the Innocent* (1954), resulted in the establishment of the Comics Code, guidelines that one comic book historian referred to as "the most severe form of censorship applied to any mass medium in the United States" (Inge 1985). The result was a decline: "Writers and artists, in an attempt to 'clean up their act,' began to grind out boring and repetitive stories about spooks and funny animals" (Brocka 1979).

The fears about comic books appeared, however, to be unfounded. Research has failed to find a strong relationship between comic book reading and behavior. Hoult (1949) reported that delinquents read more comics and more comics labeled "harmful" and "questionable" than did a comparable group of nondelinquents, but nearly all of Hoult's subjects reported reading comic books. Witty (1941) compared the 10 percent of pupils in grades four through six who read the most comics with the 10 percent who read the least, and found that the two groups "received almost the same average marks and were considered by their teachers to be about equally well-adjusted and effective in social relationships" (p. 108). Lewin (1953, cited in Witty and Sizemore 1955) reported similar results.

☐ *Comic book reading is not responsible for antisocial behavior.*

The recovery, the "Silver Age" of comic books, began in 1961, with the publication of Marvel Comics's *Fantastic Four*, followed in 1962 by what may have been the most important event in comic book history in the United States: the first appearance of Spider-Man. Under Stan Lee's leadership, Marvel developed the first superheroes with problems. Spider-Man, for example, has problems that the Superman and Batman of the 1940s and 1950s never imaged—financial problems, romance problems, lack of direction, and a lack of self-esteem.

There is clear evidence that the Silver Age is still going strong, but there have been ups and downs. Annual sales of comic books in 1983 were $200 million (*Los Angeles Herald Examiner*, October 4, 1987). This skyrocketed to $850 million in 1993 but fell to $375 million in 1998 and to $250 million in 2000 (Businessweek.com, August 29, 2002).

Some experts think the recent decline in comics is due to the development of animated computer and video games (Hartl 2003), and there are signs of recovery: In 2001, sales increased slightly to $260 million.

Movies based on comic-book characters are expected to boost interest in comics, and graphic novels or book-format comics, "meatier and fuller-length comic books" (Gorman 2002), according to one librarian, "have proven to be a hit with kids and are flying off library shelves" (Gorman 2002, p. 42), especially among teenagers. Gorman is not alone in her observations on graphic novels: The American Library Association held a preconference session on graphic novels in 2002, and BookExpo America offered a full-day graphic novel session in 2003 and had a "graphic novel pavilion" as part of the exhibitions. The *School Library Journal* now has regular columns on comics and graphic novels (see, e.g., Weiner 2003).

Just as the Marvel comics of the 1960s were a giant step beyond the comics of the 1940s, graphic novels are a giant step beyond the comic book, with subtle, complex, and often fascinating plots. Here are two graphic-novel "classics" for beginners in this genre: *The Dark Knight* (Miller 1986) features an aging Batman who comes out of retirement to fight crime, no longer in partnership with the police commissioner but as a vigilante. This Batman is tired and sore after adventures and has serious philosophical disagreements with Superman. The *Watchmen* (Moore 1986) is based on the quote from Cicero, "who watches the watchmen?" The watchmen, of course, are the superheroes. *Time Magazine* called it "the best of the breed" of graphic novels, and "a superlative feat of imagination" (Cocks 1988).

□ *Graphic novels are popular today.*

A particularly popular type of graphic novel is the Manga, Japanese graphic novels in English translation. *Publishers Weekly* described Manga as "one of the hottest categories in bookstores" (MacDonald 2003), which "is gradually evolving from a hard-core cult obsession to the kind of mainstream phenomenon that teens and young adults adopt as their own."

The number of comic books shops in the United States increased from about 100 in the mid-1970s to about 4,000 in 1987. The number has declined since the late 1980s but is still impressive. Duin (2002) reported that there were 3,600 comic book stores in the United States, and The Master List (http://www.the-master-list.com) provides information about 2,500 comic book stores in the United States and Canada.

Williams and Boyes (1986) studied children in three English-speaking Canadian communities from 1973 to 1975 and reported that 80.4 percent of the children reported that they read or had read comic books. In 1991, McKenna, Kear, and Ellsworth, using a stratified sample of children from 95 school districts in 38 states, reported that the percentage of elementary school children reading comic books in the United States was substantial: For boys, the range was from 69 percent (grade one) to 75 percent (grade 6), while for girls the range was from 50 percent (grade 6) to 60 percent (grade 1). This is less comic book readership than during the Golden Age of comics, but it is a considerable amount.

Confirming the continuing popularity of comic books, Worthy, Moorman, and Turner (1999) asked sixth graders in the Austin, Texas, area what they liked to read. The top preferences for all children, regardless of reading ability and gender, were scary books (R.L. Stine, Stephen King) and comic books.

Comic Books and Language Development

> Comic books opened up my imagination and gave me a large vocabulary ... What other six-year-old would know what a serum was? Or invulnerability? (Sharon Cho, in Rosenthal 1995, p. 51)

Wertham, in *Seduction of the Innocent* (1954), asserted that comic book reading interfered with learning to read and with language development, claiming that "severe reading difficulties and maximum comic book reading go hand in had, that far from being a help to reading, comic books are a causal and reinforcing factor in children's reading disorders" (p. 130).

Wertham's claims have not been supported. Research done on comic book texts and on the impact of comic book reading on language development and school performance suggests that comic books are not harmful. Moreover, there is considerable evidence that comic books can and do lead to more "serious" reading.

☐ *Claims that reading comic books retards reading development are unfounded.*

Comic Texts

In 1941, R. L. Thorndike recommended that comics should be considered: "In view of the need of the upper elementary school and junior high school pupil for a large volume of reading and vocabulary building experience, this source should not be neglected" (p. 110).

Current comics average about 2,000 words per issue (not counting advertisements). This is significant: One comic a day would mean well over a half million words a year, half of the average yearly reading volume of middle-class children (Anderson, Wilson, and Fielding 1988).

☐ *One comic a day = 500,000 words a year.*

Several studies of comic book reading difficulty have been done. Thorndike (1941) used the Lorge formula and reported that the popular *Superman* and *Batman* comics were written at about the fifth- or sixth-grade level. Wright (1979) used the Fry formula and evaluated a wider range of comics. Wright's findings for superhero comics (e.g., *Superman, The Incredible Hulk*) are consistent with Thorndike's, while other comics are far easier, as shown in table 2.6.[3]

Table 2.6
Reading Level of Comic Books (1978)

Title	Readability Grade Level			
	Sample 1	Sample 2	Sample 3	Mean
The Amazing Spider-Man #187	7.4	3.0	2.8	4.4
Archie #274	2.0	1.7	1.7	1.8
Batman #299	7.9	4.0	8.5	6.4
Bugs Bunny #201	2.9	1.9	1.7	2.1
Casper the Friendly Ghost #200	1.9	1.7	1.7	1.8
Chip and Dale #55	2.9	1.9	1.8	2.2
Dennis the Menace #158	2.8	3.0	4.7	3.5
The Incredible Hulk #74	5.5	9.2	1.9	5.5
Mighty Mouse #53	1.9	3.3	1.9	2.4
Sad Sack #265	2.4	1.9	1.9	2.1
Spidey Super Stories	2.7	1.8	1.9	2.1
Star Hunters #7	6.0	7.3	3.3	5.5
Star Wars #16	7.5	7.4	3.3	6.1
Superman #329	7.3	8.3	3.5	6.4
Tarzan #18	7.6	4.4	4.5	5.5
Tom and Jerry #311	1.9	2.0	1.8	1.9
Wonder Woman #245	5.5	5.5	3.5	4.8
Woody Woodpecker #172	2.4	2.4	3.0	3.1
Yogi Bear #7	3.2	3.5	2.4	3.0

Source: G. Wright, "The Comic Book: A Forgotten Medium in the Classroom," *Reading Teacher* 33 (1979). Reprinted with permission of Gary Wright and the International Reading Association.

If readability scores have any validity, Thorndike's and Wright's analyses show that comics can be at a respectable level of difficulty. In comparison, best sellers in 1974 ranged in readability from grade 6 to grade 10, with a mean readability score of 7.4 (Schulze 1976, cited in Monteith 1980).

To see how sophisticated comic dialogue can get, consider these examples. The first is from Marvel's *Fantastic Four*. In this scene Reed Richards, a master scientist (a.k.a. Mr. Fantastic), is explaining to his wife, Sue Richards (a.k.a. the Invisible Woman), how the villain Psycho-Man operates:

☐ *Comic book texts can be complex.*

> The Psycho-Man has a vast technology at his command, darling, but he had traditionally used it to only one end: to manipulate emotions. Everything he does is designed to create conflicting, confusing emotional stimuli for his intended victims. (*The Fantastic Four*, no. 283, 1985, p. 21)

The reading level of this passage, according to the Flesch-Kincaid formula, is 12.0, or 12th grade.

In Marvel's *Secret Wars*, no. 1, several superheroes speculate about how they were involuntarily transported to another planet:

> Captain Marvel: H-how'd we get here? I mean one minute we're checking out this giant watchmacallit in Central Park, then "poof," the final frontier.

> Mr. Fantastic (Reed Richards): This much I can tell you, Captain Marvel—this device apparently caused sub-atomic particle dissociation, reducing us to proto-matter, which it stored until it teleported us here, to pre-set coordinates in space, where it reassembled us inside a self-generated life support environment.

> The Incredible Hulk: That's obvious, Richards!

> (*Secret Wars*, no. 1., p. 2)

Mr. Fantastic's explanation is written at the 12th-grade level, according to the Flesch-Kincaid formula. It should be pointed out that readability formulas such as the Fry formula are based on random samples of the text. The above excerpts were not chosen at random: I selected them because they are hard. They are thus not typical of comic book language, but they show what comic books readers occasionally encounter.

Deborah Glasser has pointed out to me that if teachers are looking for high-interest/low-vocabulary reading for older students, they can't do better than *Archie*. *Archie* is about high school students, but according to Wright's data, it is written at the second-grade level. In addition, after 60 years, Archie and his friends are still in high school, certainly the longest incarceration in the history of education. This is good news for students and teachers, because it means that there are plenty of used *Archie* comics around.

The value of *Archie* comics was confirmed by Norton (2003), who studied the comic book reading habits of 30 preteen readers, all dedicated to *Archie*. The children universally praised the comics ("ARCHIE RULES") , described the characters as "interesting, engaging and humorous" (p. 142), and shared and discussed *Archie* comics with each other "on a regular basis," (p. 143), forming a true literacy community. As expected, this view was not shared by teachers and other adults. Norton asked the interesting question of when and why adults, who "loved to read Archie comics as children, dismiss them 'garbage' once they reached adulthood?" (p. 146).

☐ Archie *is excellent high-interest/ low-vocabulary reading.*

Experiments with
    Comic Book Reading

Two sustained silent reading studies using comic books have been published. In a 15-week study using fifth graders, Sperzl (1948) found no difference between groups reading comics and reading other material on tests of reading comprehension and vocabulary. Both resulted in acceptable gains. Perhaps the most interesting finding in Sperzl's study is how much the children enjoyed reading comic books. Sperzl reported that "the period was eagerly looked forward to . . . as far as the rest of the world was concerned, it simply did not exist for these boys and girls" (p. 111). (See also Norton 2003 for similar reactions to comic books among preteen readers.)

Arlin and Roth (1978) compared third graders reading "educational" (e.g., classic) comics with another group reading "high-interest" books. Both groups gained in reading comprehension. Although "poor readers" gained more from book reading, poor readers reading comic books still matched expected growth, gaining .26 years in 10 weeks.

We can interpret both studies as showing that comic book reading is at least as beneficial as other reading. Both studies, however, were short term (recall the review of in-school free reading studies done in chapter 1; in-school free reading is clearly more effective when durations are longer), and the comic book readers in Arlin and Roth's study read classic comics.[4]

A number of studies confirm that long-term comic book readers, those who continue to read comics after the early grades, are at least equal to non-comic book readers in reading, language development, and overall school achievement (Witty

1941; Heisler 1947; Blakely 1958; Swain 1948; Greaney 1980; Anderson, Wilson, and Fielding 1988). Even children who read almost nothing but comic books do not score significantly below average in reading comprehension (Greaney 1980).

An exclusive diet of comic books will probably develop adequate but not advanced levels of competence in language and literacy development. There is good evidence, however, that such reading habits are unusual. In general, long-term comic book readers do as much book reading as non-comic book readers (Witty 1941; Heisler 1947; Bailyn 1959; Swain 1948), and the results of several studies suggest they do more (Blakely 1958; Ujiie and Krashen, 1996a, 1996b).

Table 2.7 presents the results from one of these studies. Ujiie and Krashen (1996a) asked seventh-grade boys about their comic book reading, overall reading, book reading, and attitude toward reading. Those who reported more comic book reading also reported for-pleasure reading in general. The results were similar for middle class children and for "chapter 1" children, those who came from lower-income families.

Table 2.7
How Often Do You Read for Pleasure?

Chapter 1	Daily	Weekly	Monthly/never
heavy comic reader	54% (19)	34% (12)	11% (4)
occasional reader	40% (32)	28% (23)	32% (26)
non-comic reader	16% (4)	20% (5)	64% (16)
Middle Class			
heavy comic reader	65% (17)	27% (7)	8% (2)
occasional reader	35% (31)	35% (31)	30% (27)
non-comic reader	33% (8)	17% (4)	50% (12)

Source: Ujiie and Krashen (1996a)

Similar results were reported for book reading and for attitudes toward reading, with more comic book reading associated with greater enjoyment of reading. What is especially interesting is that although the middle class boys tend to read more in general, undoubtedly related to the fact that they have access to more books (Neuman and Celano 1999), heavy chapter 1 (low income) comic book readers reported more reading than the occasional and non-comic book reading middle class boys.

□ *Some studies show comic book readers read as much as non-comic book readers. Some studies show they read more.*

There is, in addition, evidence that light reading can serve as a conduit to heavier reading. It can help readers not only develop the linguistic competence for harder reading but also develop an interest in books.

□ *Comics can serve as a conduit to heavier reading.*

Comics as a Conduit

Research by Hayes and Ahrens (1988) suggests that comic books can play an important role in helping readers progress to the level where they can read and understand demanding texts. According to their findings, it is highly unlikely that much educated vocabulary comes from conversation or television. Hayes and Ahrens found that the frequency of less-common words in ordinary conversation, whether adult-to-child or adult-to- adult, was much lower than in even the "lightest" reading. About 95 percent of the words used in conversation and television are among the most frequent 5,000 words. Printed texts include far more uncommon words, leading Hayes and Ahrens to the conclusion that the development of lexical knowledge beyond basic words "requires literacy and extensive reading across a broad range of subjects" (p. 409). Table 2.8 presents some of their data, including two of the three measures they used for word frequency.

Note that comic books occupy a position between conversation and abstracts of scientific papers, falling somewhat closer to conversation. This confirms that they can serve as a conduit to more challenging reading.

Table 2.8
Common and Uncommon Words in Speech and Writing

	Frequent Words	Rare Words
Adults talking to children	95.6	9.9
Adults talking to adults (college grads)	93.9	17.3
Prime-time TV: adult	94.0	22.7
Children's books	92.3	30.9
Comic books	88.6	53.5
Books	88.4	52.7
Popular magazines	85.0	65.7
Newspapers	84.3	68.3
Abstracts of scientific papers	70.3	128.2

frequent words = percentage of text from most frequent 5,000 words
rare words = number of rare words (not in most common 10,000) per 1,000 tokens.
Source: Hayes and Ahrens (1988)

Several case histories support the view that light reading is the way many, if not most, children learn to read and develop a taste for reading.

Haugaard (1973) writes of her experiences with comic books:

> As the mother of three boys, who, one after another, were notoriously unmotivated to read and had to be urged, coaxed, cajoled, threatened and drilled in order even to stay in super slow group in reading, I wish to thank comic books for being a conduit, if not a contribution, to culture.

The first thing which my oldest boy read because he wanted to was a comic book. (p. 84)

Despite her initial reluctance, Haugaard
bought her son comics, reasoning that

as long as these things appealed to him where all
other printed matter had failed, I let him read all
he wanted. The words he learned to read here
could be used in other reading material too and
perhaps his skill would lure him beyond this
level. (p. 84)

The results were startling:

He devoured what seemed to be tons of the
things . . . The motivation these comics provided
was absolutely phenomenal and a little bit
frightening. My son would snatch up a new one
and, with feverish and ravenous eyes, start gob-
bling it wherever he was—in the car on the way
home from the market, in the middle of the yard,
walking down the street, at the dinner table. All
his senses seemed to shut down and he became
a simple visual pipeline. (p. 85)

☐ *Comic books lead to
other reading.*

Comics did indeed lead to other reading. After
a year or two, Haugaard's eldest son gave his collection away to his younger brother (who now
"pores over the comic books lovingly"), and
Haugaard noted that "he is far more interested now
in reading Jules Verne and Ray Bradbury, books on
electronics and science encyclopedias" (p. 85).

Haugaard's experience is consistent with the
rest of the literature. Her sons' absorption in comics is identical to the reaction Sperzl's students had
(see "Experiments with Comic Book Reading"
above), and the eldest son's interest in other kinds
of reading agrees with the studies mentioned earlier showing that comic book reading does not re-
place or eliminate book reading. (It should be

pointed out that the results of these studies suggest that Haugaard's eldest son need not have given up comics in order to enjoy other books. He might not have stopped if he had access to today's graphic novels.)

Mark Mathabane, in his autobiographical account of his youth in South Africa (Mathabane 1986), mentions comic books as making an important contribution to his acquisition of English and his desire to read. Mathabane had had limited exposure to English until his grandmother began to work for a friendly English-speaking family outside the impoverished ghetto were Mathabane and his family lived:

□ *Autobiographical examples attest to the value of comic book reading.*

> Not long after she started working for the Smiths, she began bringing home stacks of comic books: *Batman and Robin, Richie Rich, Dennis the Menace, The Justice League of America, Tarzan of the Apes, Sherlock Holmes, Mysteries, Superman, The Incredible Hulk, Thor—God of Thunder, The Fantastic Four* and *Spider-Man.* (p. 170)

Mathabane's reaction was similar to that of Haugaard's son:

> Having never owned a comic book in my life, I tirelessly read them over and over again, the parts I could understand. Such voracious reading was like an anesthesia, numbing me to the harsh life around me. Soon comic books became the joy of my life, and everywhere I went I took one with me: to the river, to a soccer game, to the lavatory, to sleep, to the store and to school, reading it furtively when the teacher was busy at the blackboard. (p. 170)

Mathabane credits comics with helping to bring his English to a level where he could begin to read and appreciate his English books:

> Midway into my eleventh year, Granny started
> bringing home strange-looking books and toys.
> The books, which she said were Mrs. Smith's
> son's schoolbooks, bore no resemblance what-
> soever to the ones we used at my school. Their
> names were as strange to me as their contents:
> *Pinnocchio, Aesop's Fables* and fairy tales of the
> brothers Grimm. At this point, because of read-
> ing comics, my English had improved to a level
> where I could read simple sentences. I found the
> books enthralling. (p. 170)

Comics also helped South Africa's Bishop
Desmond Tutu:

> My father was the headmaster of a Methodist
> primary school. Like most fathers in those days,
> he was very patriarchal, very concerned that we
> did well in school. But one of the things I am
> very grateful to him for is that, contrary to con-
> ventional educational principles, he allowed me
> to read comics. I think that is how I developed
> my love for English and for reading. (Campbell
> and Hayes, cited in Trelease 2001, p. 134)

Trelease (2001) points out that anybody concerned about a possible connection between
comic book reading and juvenile delinquency
should consider Bishop Tutu's experience.

M. Thomas Inge, a professor of the humani-
ties, remarks that comics were clearly a conduit for
him and others: "For my generation, it was the
comic book that led directly to the printed page"
(Inge 1985, p. 5). Professor Inge has clearly not
given up reading comics. His essays on comic
books (Inge 1985) are informative and scholarly.

□ *"For my generation, it was the comic book that led directly to the printed page."*

This writer's experience is similar: I was in the
low reading group in the second grade. My father
encouraged comic book reading, and improvement soon followed. And Jim Trelease tells us that
as a child, he had the largest comic book collection

in his neighborhood (Trelease 2001, p. 134). His conclusion, based on the research and his personal experience is that "if you have a child who is struggling with reading, connect him or her with comics. If an interest appears, feed it with more comics" (p. 134).

Dorrell and Carroll (1981) show how comic books can be used to stimulate additional reading. They placed comic books in a junior high school library but did not allow them to circulate; students had to come to the library to read the comics. Dorrell and Carroll then compared the circulation of non-comic book material and total library use during the 74 days the comics were in the library, and the 57 days before they were available. The presence of comics resulted in a dramatic 82 percent increase in library use (traffic) and a 30 percent increase in circulation of non-comic material (table 2.9).

Table 2.9
Effects of Including Comic Books
in a Junior High School Library

	Pre-comic Period	Comic Period
Number of students who used the library (daily average)	272.61	496.38
Circulation (daily average)	77.49	100.99

Pre-comic period = 54 days; comic period = 74 days

Number of students who used the library does not include students brought to the library by teachers for class assignments.

Source: Adapted from L. Dorrell and E. Carroll, "Spider-Man at the Library," *School Library Journal* 27 (1981).

Dorrell and Carroll also reported that the presence of comics in the library did not result in any negative comments from parents, and that teachers, school administrators, and library staff members supported and encouraged the idea of comic books in the library.

Juan Necochea, now a professional academic, related how comics contributed to his literacy development (Cline and Necochea 2003). Necochea began school at age eight in the United States, with no knowledge of English and no previous schooling. Yet, "toward the end of the second grade, at the age of 9, . . . there was a sudden a significant surge in my academic performance—I seemed to go from a nonreader to proficient reader of English practically overnight . . . my teachers . . . must have assumed that I must have been a 'late bloomer' " (p. 124).

Necochea attributes his success to his previously developed literacy in Spanish, which, he informs us, came from two sources: A home environment rich in oral language, filled with "folk tales, legends, family histories, tragedies, music and traditions" (p.124), and . . . comics books. Necochea was an avid comic book reader (his favorite was *Kalimán, el Hombre Increíble*). At first he paid his older brother to read the comics to him, but eventually he learned to read them himself: "*Kalimán* and my older brother became my first reading teachers" (p. 125). Necochea reports that by age six he could read in Spanish very well.

This case not only confirms the power of comic books, it also confirms the power of first language literacy as a facilitator of second language literacy, a topic we return to in chapter 3.

The Case for Comics

The case for comics is a good one:

- The texts of comics are linguistically appropriate, and pictures can help make the texts comprehensible.[5]

- Research shows that comics have no negative effect on language development and school achievement.

- Comic book readers do at least as much reading as non-comic book readers, and the most recent research shows that they read more overall, read more books, and have more positive attitudes toward reading.

- There is strong evidence from case studies that comics can serve as a conduit to book reading.

Light Reading: The Teen Romance

Another example of light reading that can encourage additional reading is the teen romance. Parrish (1983) provides this characterization:

> Most of teen romance books are written to a formula. The central character is a girl, 15 to 16 years old, and the story is always told from her viewpoint. One or more boys, 17 to 18 years old, are also needed. The setting is usually contemporary and familiar, such as a small town. First love is a favorite plot focus.
>
> The joys of falling in love, the anxiety it engenders, the pain and growth of problems met, and the inevitable happy ending are all standard. However, these romances exclude sexual situations, profanity, or perversions. The conflict is usually about the heroine's feelings—insecurity, uncertainty, unpopularity, inferiority, pleasure/pain, a struggle for independence. Dialogue generally carries the action, while characterization is revealed through the romantic interaction and problems. (p. 611)

Teen romances were read by many, if not most, girls in junior high school and high school in the 1980s. Parrish and Atwood (1985) surveyed 250 junior and senior high school girls in the Phoenix metropolitan area and reported that during the school year, 50 percent of the eighth graders said they had read from one to five teen romances, and 100 percent of the ninth graders had read at least five. Also, "an astonishing 12% of the twelfth graders had read in excess of thirty novels this school year" (p. 24).

□ *Teen romances are very popular with teenage girls.*

Although there has been little research on teen romances, the results are quite similar to those of comic book research.

Teen romances appear to have linguistically acceptable texts, ranging in reading level from grade four to grade seven. *Sweet Valley Twins* is written at the fourth-grade reading level; *Sweet Dream Romances*, written for girls ages 10 to 15, is at the fifth-grade level; and the *Sweet Valley High* series, for age 12 and older, is written at the sixth-grade level. *Caitlin*, a "love trilogy" written by Francine Pascal, ranges from the grade five to the grade seven reading level. By way of comparison, recall that the mean readability level of best sellers is around the seventh-grade level.

□ *Reading levels range from grades four to seven.*

Reading teen romances does not seem to prevent other kinds of reading. Parrish and Atwood (1985) found that "students who read the romance novels read many other kinds of literature also" (p. 25).

Teen romances appear to bring students into the library. According to Parrish and Atwood, eighth and ninth graders in the 1980s got their romance novels equally from friends, bookstores, and school libraries. Tenth graders favored drug and grocery stories and the school library. Twelfth graders showed the greatest diversity: Over half got their books from friends and the public library, 37 percent from bookstores and the school library, with little use of home and drug/grocery stores. Thus, despite the existence of other places to get teen romances, the school library still plays a significant role as a source of reading for this genre.

There is evidence that reading teen romances promotes reading. The following, quoted by Parrish (1983), sounds very much like Haugaard's report of how comic books stimulate reading. The writer is a 14-year-old girl: "I am the kind of person who hates to read, but when my mother brought home a Silhouette book for me to read, I just couldn't put it down" (p. 615)

□ *There is no research on the behavioral effects of reading teen romances.*

Just as there has been concern about the content of comic books, there is concern about the content of teen romances. There has been no research on the behavioral effects of teen romances, but concerned teachers and parents may be interested in reading Sutton's thoughtful review. Sutton (1985) gives the teen romance cautious approval, suggesting that while we regard "the lesser lights of paperback fiction as the competition" (p. 29), they have some merit:

> Characterization is minimal, the writing is less than graceful ("They were all being so polite and civilized the twins thought they would throw up.") and even romance is overshadowed by the soap opera suspense. But it does work: the bare bones plots, hokey and hoary, move. The links between successive volumes are clever, and you really want to know . . . what Jessica is going to pull next (p. 27).

□ *Teen romances worked for some adult second language acquirers.*

A recent series of studies suggests that teen romances may have another important use: They may be ideal sources of comprehensible and interesting reading material for some acquirers of English as a second language.

Kyung-Sook Cho (Cho and Krashen 1994, 1995a, 1995b) worked with a group of women in their thirties who, despite years of formal (grammar-based) study of English in Korea and considerable residence in the United States, had made little progress in English. Cho first suggested that her subjects read books from the *Sweet Valley High* series, written for girls ages 12 and older. These books proved to be too difficult; they could only be read with great effort, and with extensive recourse to the dictionary. Cho then asked her subjects to try *Sweet Valley Twins*, novels based on the same characters but at a younger age, written for readers ages 8 to 12. Once again, the texts were too difficult. Cho then recommended *Sweet Valley Kids*, novels dealing with the same characters at an even younger age, written for readers ages five to eight. Her subjects, all adults, became enthusiastic *Sweet Valley Kids* readers.

Cho reported significant vocabulary growth in her readers (Cho and Krashen 1994), and also gathered informal evidence of their progress, including reports from their friends (Cho and Krashen 1995a). Perhaps the most impressive result is the report of one of her subjects one year after she starting reading *Sweet Valley* books. After one year, this subject, who had never read for pleasure in English prior to this study, had read all 34 *Sweet Valley Kids* books, had read many books from the *Sweet Valley Twins* and *Sweet Valley High* series, and had started to read Danielle Steele, Sydney Sheldon, and other authors of romances in English (Cho and Krashen 1995a).

Light Reading: The Power of Magazines

Rucker (1982) provides a strong demonstration of the power of magazines to promote and improve reading ability. Rucker gave junior high

□ *Magazine reading appears to promote more reading.*

school students questionnaires probing their interests. A few months later, he provided a random sample of the students with two free magazine subscriptions relating to their interests. One group of students received the magazines for one year, another for a year and a half. Neither the students nor their parents were informed that an experiment was being conducted, and even teachers did not know about the subscriptions.

Rucker reported that students who received the magazines had superior gains on standardized tests of reading (but not on a test of "language," i.e., mechanics and spelling). A reasonable interpretation of these results is that the magazines themselves served as valuable input and that they stimulated even more reading. As Rucker points out, magazines are the most "reader interest specific" of all mass media and "may thus consequently be the most valuable as stimuli to reading" (p. 33).

Is Light Reading Enough?

□ *A diet of light reading only isn't enough.*

It is sensible to suppose that what is read matters. Despite the benefits of light reading, a diet of only light reading will probably not lead to advanced levels of development. Only a few studies bear on this issue, and they are correlational, which means we cannot be sure whether reading preferences are a cause or result (or both) of reading ability. The studies, however, suggest that reading comprehension and vocabulary development are related to what is read.

Rice (1986) reported that adults with better vocabularies "tended to read more sophisticated materials," such as technical journals, history, literary magazines, and science magazines. Hafner,

Palmer, and Tullos (1986) found that better readers (top one-half on a reading comprehension test) in the ninth grade tended to prefer "complex fiction" (historical fiction, science fiction, mystery, adventure, personal development, personal insight), while "poor readers" (bottom one-half) tended to prefer "how-to-do-it" books, science books, hobby books, and books on art, music, and history. Southgate, Arnold, and Johnson (1981) found that seven- to nine-year-olds who were better readers preferred adventure books, while "funny books" were more popular with less advanced readers.

Thorndike (1973), in his large-scale study of reading comprehension in 15 countries, reported that for 14-year-olds the types of reading that correlated best with reading comprehension ability were, in order, 1) humor; 2) history and biography; 3) science fiction, myths, and legends; and 3) adventure and current events. Thorndike also reported that by the end of secondary school the pattern had changed somewhat: While reading of sports, love stories, and school stories was negatively correlated with reading comprehension, history and biography, technical science, and philosophy and religion showed the strongest positive correlation.

There is some agreement among the studies; science fiction and adventure books seem to be consistently preferred by good readers. There are also some contradictions: Good readers, according to Thorndike, prefer history and religious books, but in the Hafner, Palmer, and Tullos study, poor readers preferred these topics. (An obvious problem in relating reading growth to genre is that there might be quite a bit of variation in complexity within one kind of reading. Clearly, research in this area has just begun.)

As noted earlier, Greaney (1980) identified a group of "predominately comic book readers," fifth-grade children who did far more comic book reading than book reading. These children were not significantly below the group average in reading comprehension but were not as proficient as children classified as "predominately book readers."

The results of these studies do not imply that light reading is to be avoided. As argued earlier, light reading can serve as a conduit to heavier reading: It provides both the motivation for more reading and the linguistic competence that makes harder reading possible. Reassuring and supporting evidence comes from studies that show that many children who do extensive free reading eventually choose what experts have decided are "good books" (Schoonover 1938), and studies show that readers gradually expand their reading interests as they read more (LaBrant 1958). Also, books children select on their own are often harder than their official "reading level" (Southgate, Arnold, and Johnson 1981).

☐ *Light reading isn't enough, but it can lead to heavier reading*

Do Rewards Work?

The studies presented in this chapter suggest that the intrinsic reward of reading is so great that it will stimulate additional reading. They suggest that we do not need extrinsic rewards for reading, that is, gold stars, cash awards, reading club membership, or other incentives. Smith (1988) argues, in fact, that awards can backfire:

> Show a child that the payoff for reading or writing something is a treat, a token, a happy face or a high mark, and that is what the child will learn is the price literacy should extract. Every child knows that anything accomplished by coercion, no matter how benign, cannot be worth doing it its own right. (p. 124)

What Does the Research Say?

Research offers no support for the use of rewards and suggests, in agreement with Smith, that rewards may be harmful.

McLoyd (1979) asked second and third graders to read from "high-interest" books under three conditions: "high reward," "low reward," and "no reward." In the high reward condition, children were promised a reward that they rated the most highly out of six presented. In the low reward condition, children were promised a reward that they rated the least highly out of six presented.

It was explained to the rewarded children that the reward would be granted if they read until they reached a marker in the book indicating 250 words and that the experimenter was interested in their opinion of the book. Rewards were not mentioned to the children in the no reward condition; rather, they were simply asked to read up to the indicated place in the text and to then give their opinion of the book. The reading sessions lasted 10 minutes.

□ *Rewarding reading sends the message that reading is unpleasant or not worth doing without a reward.*

The difference between the two rewarded groups was not statistically significant, but both rewarded groups differed from the non-rewarded group. The rewarded groups clearly read only what they had to in order to get the reward, barely going beyond the 250-word marker. The non-rewarded readers went well beyond this point; they read more than twice as much as the rewarded groups.

Children appear to be perfectly willing to read without rewards (witness the success of Harry Potter) and do not even think of rewards when asked about how to encourage reading, in contrast to teachers.

Worthy (2000) asked 419 middle school children and 35 teachers for their suggestions for motivating students to read. The schools were from a range of ethnic and socioeconomic groups.

The students were asked: "What could your language arts teacher do to make students more motivated to read?" Students were asked to write up to three suggestions, and made a total of 509 suggestions. Teachers were asked, "What do you think are the best ways of motivating students to read?" and provided "multiple suggestions." Both groups recommended providing more interesting books (students = 45 percent of suggestions, teachers = 35 percent), and both recommended more student choice and more read-alouds. Nine student suggestions were for more time to read, but this was not mentioned by teachers.

Of interest to us here is incentives: "Teachers and students made strikingly different suggestions regarding incentives. Although 29% of teacher suggestions were focused on rewarding or coercing students to read (i.e. grades, "nagging") only 9% of students' suggestions fell into this category, and often their suggestions were obviously facetious (e.g. 'Give us $10 for every page we read)" (p. 448).

□ *When asked how to encourage reading, students rarely recommend rewards.*

Worthy noted that, "Although most teachers spoke of the importance of developing intrinsic motivation to read, more than half said that they used external motivators as inducements to reading" (p. 448).

Similarly, Ivey and Broaddus (2001) asked 1,765 sixth graders what stimulated them to read; only 7 percent mentioned external rewards.

Bintz (1993) also found that many teachers believed in incentives. He asked teachers what would promote student interest in reading. Teachers felt that many students were not interested in reading and that they needed to be forced to read and needed to be "held accountable" for their reading. Many of the teachers, Bintz concluded, were unaware that many of these "reluctant" readers were avid readers of self-selected reading outside of school. The students, according to Bintz, were not reluctant to read but were only reluctant to read school-assigned material.

Reading Management Programs

A number of studies have attempted to determine the impact of reading management programs, programs in which children are tested on what they read and rewarded for points earned on these tests. McQuillan (1997) reviewed studies of the effectiveness of these programs and concluded that there was no evidence that they improved reading achievement or attitudes toward reading. I have recently reviewed studies of the best known of these programs, Accelerated Reader (Krashen 2003d), and summarize my results here.

Accelerated Reader (AR) has four components:

1.   Children are provided with substantial access to books.

2.   Children read books that they select themselves (AR recommends one hour per day for free voluntary reading).

3.   Children earn points by taking tests on the content of the books, tests that focus on literal meaning.

4.   Children get prizes in exchange for the points they earn on the tests. (The AR company points out that this feature is not intrinsic to AR, but is at the discretion of the school.)

We would not be surprised to learn that a program that includes items 1 and 2 will increase reading proficiency. As discussed in this chapter, there is strong evidence that when readers are provided access to comprehensible and interesting reading material, they read more. As documented in chapter 1, those who read more, read better. The question of interest, then, is whether features 3 and 4 make any difference. Do tests and rewards help? The obvious study that would settle this is to see whether programs such as Accelerated Reader are better than simply providing more books and more time to read. Unfortunately, this kind of comparison has not been done.

□ *Studies of Accelerated Reader do not provide evidence that tests and rewards are helpful.*

Studies of Accelerated Reader

Most studies of the efficacy of AR compare AR to doing nothing special; that is, they compare students in AR programs to students in traditional language arts classes in which no effort is made to increase access to books, encourage reading, and provide more time to read. Many of the results are positive, with AR students doing better on standardized tests than comparison students in traditional language arts classes. Even when results are positive, however, they do not tell us which aspects of AR are responsible for the results. I reviewed these studies in detail in Krashen (2003d).

Not all of these studies, however, show that AR was in fact more effective than traditional language arts instruction. Goodman (1999) reported that AR students gained only three months over an academic year on standardized tests of reading comprehension. In one of the reports on the official AR Web site (renlearn.com; Report 36), AR was done in two middle school classrooms for one year. One class showed gains, the other did not: Mathis (1996) compared progress with AR for a group of sixth graders with gains made by the same students the year before and found no difference. It could be argued that the duration of these studies was not long enough to show the impact of AR: Recall that the impact of sustained silent reading is greater when studies are long term. This does not help explain the results of the next study, however.

Pavonetti, Brimmer, and Cipielewski (2003) administered the Title Recognition Test to seventh graders in three districts. The Title Recognition Test is a checklist that correlates highly with other measures of reading exposure as well as with various measures of reading achievement (see discussion in "The Author Recognition Test" section in chapter 1). For all three districts combined, Pavonetti et al. reported no difference between those children who had had AR and those who had not.

Only three studies have attempted to deal with the issue of what aspect of AR is effective. In all three, however, it appears to be the case that the AR group had more exposure to comprehensible text, and in two studies the comparison group did not do pure "recreational reading." In all three studies, the results are inconsistent and unclear.[6]

Conclusions on AR

Despite the popularity of AR, we must conclude that there is no real evidence supporting it, no real evidence that the additional tests and rewards add anything to the power of simply supplying access to high-quality and interesting reading material and providing time for children to read.

This is not to say that I have proven that AR is ineffective. I have only concluded that data supporting it do not exist. Although McLoyd's results suggest that rewards actually inhibit reading, we must withhold judgment until additional controlled studies confirm this. What we can conclude, however, is that the enthusiasm for AR is not supported by research. Before purchasing AR and submitting students to tests, a more prudent policy might be to ensure that high-interest reading material is easily available to students, and that students have time to read and a place to read.[7]

Notes

1. These results are summarized below. In all cases, poverty was a significant predictor of achievement. The number of books per student and amount of library staffing were also consistent predictors of achievement. In some studies, these relationships held even when poverty was controlled, but in others they were only present when poverty was not controlled.

Predictors of Test Score Performance

Study	Colo. II	Alaska	Pa.	Oreg.	Tex.	Ind.	Mass.	Iowa
	RC	RC, LA, M	RC	RC	RC	lit, M	LA, M, Sc	RC
poverty	yes	yes	contr.	yes	yes	contr.	yes	yes
books	yes*	no	no	yes*	yes	yes	yes	yes**
staffing	yes*	yes**	yes	yes*	yes	yes	yes	yes**

* = books and staffing combined as one factor

** = differences emerge if poverty not controlled

RC = reading comprehension

contr. = statistically controlled

lit = literacy; M = math; Sc = science; LA = language arts

Sources: Colorado II = Lance, Rodney, and Hamilton-Pennell (2000a); Alaska = Lance, Hamilton-Pennell, Rodney, Petersen, and Sitter (1999); Pennsylvania = Lance, Rodney, and Hamilton-Pennell (2000b); Oregon = Lance, Rodney, and Hamilton-Pennell (2001); Texas = Smith (2001); Indiana = NCES (2000); Massachusetts = Baughman (2000); Iowa = Rodney, Lance, and Hamilton-Pennell (2002).

2. For additional arguments against the overemphasis on phonemic awareness and phonics, see Krashen (2002, 2003b); Smith (1994b).

3. The Fry formula is based on three random samples of 100 words. These samples can vary quite a bit. Note, for example, the variability in the three samples for *The Incredible Hulk* in table 2.2 (5.5, 9.2, 1.9). Daniel Krashen has suggested to me that the 9.2 sample may have been based on the speech of Bruce Banner, the Hulk's alter ego. Banner is a research scientist, and his speech reflects his profession.

4. Although classic comics are probably more acceptable to parents and teachers, there is evidence that they are not all that popular with children. Wayne (1954) asked 297 seventh-grade students to indicate which comic types they preferred; each student was asked to choose four from a list of 15. Classic comics ranked ninth out of 15. When children are asked which comics they prefer, without a list to choose from, classic comics are never mentioned (for a review of these studies, see Witty and Sizemore 1954). Michael Dirda, in his reading autobiography, shares his enthusiasm for comic books, but tells us, "I never really cottoned to the earnest and didactic 'classic comics'. . . . Who would pick up something called *The Cloister and the Hearth*?" (Dirda 2003, p. 56).

5. There has been some concern that the pictures in comic books will allow children to ignore the text and might actually interfere with learning to read (Wertham 1954). According to language acquisition theory, however, pictures can actually help, because they can provide clues that shed light on the meaning of an unfamiliar word or grammatical structure—they can, in other words, help make texts more comprehensible (Krashen

1985). As one comic book reader, a preteen acquirer of English as a second language, put it: "[T]hey got picture . . . colorful picture to help the readers to understand like how, what is happening, going on" (Guofang, quoted in Norton 2003, p. 143).

But some children do ignore the text and only look at the pictures. Bailyn (1959) found that 27 percent of the fifth- and sixth-grade boys she observed reading comic books "concentrated mainly on the pictures." In their sustained silent reading study, Arlin and Roth (1978) reported that poor readers appeared to do more picture reading of comic books than good readers did.

Why are some children picture readers? At first glance, the picture reading syndrome is puzzling, because pictures do not tell the whole story in most comics, and children do not typically ignore print in their environment. Here are some possibilities:

A difficult text combined with attractive pictures. While readers can tolerate some "noise" in texts, too many unknown elements will discourage attempts at comprehension (Frebody and Anderson 1983). A second grader may not even try to read the relatively complex text and storyline of comics such as *X-Men* or *Negation*, but might find the pictures of great interest.

Mistaken assumptions about reading. Some picture readers may be able to read substantial portions of the text but do not attempt to read. It is possible that their incorrect assumptions about reading discourage these children from trying to read. Because of "reading lessons" in school, they may have the mistaken impression that in order to read they need to know every word in the text. Such an assumption sets up a defeating sequence of events: The reader reads less, and as a result has less of a chance to develop reading ability and acquire more language.

These are only possibilities. Frank Smith has pointed out to me that if they are true, it does not follow that picture reading can be cured by denying the child comic books. More comic reading, not less, may be the solution. With more exposure, the child's interest in the story might stimulate attempts at reading.

6. One report appears in two versions: Vollands, Topping, and Evans (1996) is an ERIC report, while Vollands, Topping, and Evans (1999) is a slightly abbreviated version appearing in *The Reading and Writing Quarterly*. The report included two independent studies, each lasting six months. In both cases, it is claimed that AR was compared to a group that did recreational reading.

Vollands, Topping, and Evans: Project A: As discussed in detail in Krashen (2003d), this study provides no clear support for AR. The comparison group children had to give "written feedback" on what they read, and the AR group was read to in addition to doing self-selected reading. Jeff McQuillan (personal communication) has pointed out that if we add the read-aloud time to the SSR times, the AR group had considerably more exposure to comprehensible text, 3,225 minutes compared to 2,850 minutes for the comparison group. As noted earlier in this chapter, read-alouds contribute strongly to literacy development

The results are not clear. The AR group made better gains on one measure of reading comprehension as well as on a test of reading accuracy, but both groups declined on another test of reading comprehension, given only to a random subsample of the AR group. The AR group appeared to decline less, however, than the comparison group did.

This study is not a comparison of AR versus recreational reading alone. It is a comparison of two programs in which students in both programs were held accountable for what they read, and the children in the AR group had more exposure to comprehensible text than comparison children did.

Vollands et al.: Project B: The comparison group in this study was also engaged in an incentive program. Vollands et al. noted that that "children would write their name on a publicly displayed chart when they had finished their book" (1999, p. 54). In addition, comparison children also read from a selection of novels, with all reading done aloud by the students, and they had to answer comprehension questions on the reading. This is not free voluntary reading. If we only consider the genuine free reading done by the comparison group, the AR children had slightly more exposure to comprehensible text (see Krashen 2003d for details).

AR children in this study took tests but did not receive rewards. Points earned, however, were displayed in public.

The results were inconsistent. Comparison students made larger gains on one standardized test of reading comprehension (Edinburgh), but AR students made larger gains on another reading comprehension measure (Neale), with comparisons making no gains at all on the Neale, a mysterious result, because comparisons were considered to be "good readers." This inconsistency may be due to the fact that all 26 comparison students and nearly all AR students took the Edinburgh test, but only a random sample of 11 AR students and 12 comparison students took the Neale comprehension test.

It is difficult to conclude much of anything from this study: Both groups had similar incentives (recognition), and results were mixed.

Facemire (2000) also used a comparison group that was engaged in recreational reading. AR was used with 15 third graders in a high poverty area of West Virginia. AR students gained five months over the nine-week period, and comparisons gained three months. This study is an important step in the right direction but has a few problems. First, it is likely that the AR students read more than the comparisons did; AR students had "at least" 20 minutes per day of SSR, while comparisons had exactly 20 minutes. While comparisons had "access" to the library, AR students had a regularly scheduled 80 minutes per week.

Second, each group contained one unusual outlier. The AR group included one child who gained 2.3 years in nine weeks, and the comparison group included one child who got much worse in reading, dropping more than one year during the nine-week study. If we remove these outliers, the groups look nearly the same, with the AR group gaining four months and the comparisons three and one-half months.

7. A study of EFL students in Japan (Kitao, Yamamoto, Kitao, and Shimatani 1990) contains some interesting statistics that show that the usual means of encouraging reading don't work very well. They compared reading graded readers as a course requirement with reading graded readers for extra credit. All students had to hand in book reports to receive credit. Two hundred twenty graded readers were made available.

Those who read as a requirement read only what was assigned: 92 out the 93 students did the assigned reading, but 87 of them read only one book. Only 69 out of the 207 who were offered extra credit handed in book reports. Of those who handed in reports, the average was slightly more than two per student (2.2).

Why these sad results? There are several possibilities:

1.   The book report requirement made reading much less desirable.

2.   The books were simply not interesting: Even though students rated the books as somewhat interesting (mean of 4.44 on a 1 to 6 scale), "interest" was not the reason the readers read. When the readers were asked what motivated them to read, only five listed "interesting books" as their first reason, and only 17 listed this as their second reason.

3.   The students had little time to read outside of school. When the nonreaders were asked why they did not read, 70 out of 128 indicated they were too busy as their first reason, and 37 more mentioned this as their second reason.

What we can conclude is that for university students, reading graded readers for grades or extra credit, with required book reports, does not produce spectacular results.

Other Issues and Conclusions 3

The Limits of Reading

Even with massive free voluntary reading of appropriate texts, complete acquisition of the conventions of writing may not take place; even very well-read people may have gaps in their competence. Typically, these gaps are small, and many readers will recognize them as problems they experience. Here are some examples:

□ *Even with extensive FVR, gaps in literacy may remain.*

Spelling demons: Words like "committment" (or is it "commitment"?) and "independence" (or is it "independance"?).

Punctuation: Does the comma go inside or outside the quotation mark?

Grammar: Subject-verb agreement is sentences such as: A large group of boys is (are?) expected to arrive tomorrow.

These errors usually do not make much of a difference in terms of communication. "Independance," for example, communicates the idea just as well as "independence." Obeying the rules, however, is important for cosmetic reasons; readers often find written language containing errors irritating, and this reaction can detract from a writer's message.

Why do well-read readers have gaps? What prevents the full acquisition of the written language? One explanation is that not all the print is attended to; that is, successful reading for meaning does not require the full use of everything that appears on the page. It has been demonstrated (Goodman, in Flurkey and Xu 2003; Smith 1994b) that fluent readers generate hypotheses about the text they are about to read, based on what they have read already, their knowledge of the world, and their knowledge of language, and only attend to those aspects of print they need to confirm their hypotheses. For example, most readers can guess what the last word of this sentence is going to __. Good readers don't need to fully and carefully perceive the "be" at the end of the sentence in order to understand it; they just need to see enough to confirm that it is there.

☐ *Good readers do not attend to everything on the page.*

Thus, competent readers do not pay attention to every detail on the page, and they may fail to acquire the its/it's distinction or whether certain words end in -ence or -ance. These tiny gaps, in my view, are a small price to pay for fluent and efficient reading.[1]

Even those aspects of print that are attended to and understood may not be acquired. Several researchers have hypothesized that affective factors may be responsible for failure to acquire some aspects of language. Dulay and Burt (1977; see also Dulay, Burt, and Krashen 1982) have suggested that for language acquisition to occur, language acquirers need to be "open" to the input, or have a low "Affective Filter." When language acquirers are anxious, or put on the defensive, the input may be understood, but it will not reach those parts of the brain that are responsible for language acquisition (what Chomsky has called the "language acquisition device"; see Chomsky 1965). A block, the Affective Filter, will keep the input out.

☐ *The "affective filter" prevents input from reaching the "language acquisition device."*

Smith (1988) has pointed out that a great deal of learning occurs effortlessly, when learners consider themselves to be potential members of certain groups, or "clubs," and expect to learn. Teenagers, for example, learn the elaborate dress code, slang, and behavior patterns of their peers not by deliberate study but by observing others and deciding they want to be like them. Similarly, Smith argues, when readers conclude that they are potential members of the "literacy club," people who read and write, they "read like writers" and absorb the enormous amount of knowledge that writers possess. Smith's idea is quite consistent with the Affective Filter hypothesis: Considering oneself a member or potential member of the literacy club results in a lower Affective Filter, with more of the input reaching the language acquisition device.[2]

□ *When readers consider themselves to be potential members of "the literacy club," they acquire the enormous amount of information that writers possess.*

What can be done to fill these tiny gaps, those that remain even after massive reading and after entrance into the literacy club? We do, unfortunately, need to be concerned, because society's standards for writing accuracy are 100 percent. Errors in spelling, punctuation, and grammar are not tolerated in writing intended to be read by others, unless it is informal e-mail.

□ *Direct teaching can help fill some of the gap.*

Direct teaching and the use of grammar handbooks and dictionaries can help us fill at least part of the gap. Such conscious learning of language is very limited, however, and needs to be used with caution—an excessive concern with form or correctness while trying to work out new ideas in writing can be very disruptive. Experienced writers know this and limit their "editing" to the final draft, after their ideas have been worked out on the page (see, e.g., Sommers 1980). It also seems reasonable to expect that only more mature students

131

will be able to develop extensive conscious knowledge; it might be most efficient to delay this kind of direct teaching until high school.

Given extensive free reading, however, and a genuine invitation to join the literacy club, readers will acquire nearly all of the conventions of writing. With enough reading, good grammar, good spelling, and good style will be part of them, absorbed or acquired effortlessly.

Writing

Writing deserves more space than I am giving it here. My goal, however, is not to provide a complete survey of what is known about writing and how writing ability develops, but to make two crucial points:

1. Writing style does not come from actual writing experience, but from reading.

2. Actual writing can help us solve problems and make us smarter.

Writing Style Comes from Reading

The research reviewed earlier strongly suggests that we learn to write by reading. To be more precise, we acquire writing style, the special language of writing, by reading. We have already seen plenty of evidence that this is so: In chapter 1 we saw that those who participate in free reading programs write better (e.g., Elley and Mangubhai 1983; McNeil in Fader 1976), and those who report they read more write better (e.g., Applebee 1978; Alexander 1986; Salyer 1987; Janopoulous 1986; Kaplan and Palhinda 1981; Applebee, Langer, Mullis, Jenkins, and Foertsch 1990). As noted in chapter 1, Lee and Krashen (1996) and Lee (2001) have confirmed that more reading is related to better writing in Chinese (Mandarin).

There are other reasons to suspect that writing style comes from reading. The "complexity argument" (see chapter 1) applies to writing as well. All the ways in which "formal" written language differs from informal conversational language are too complex to be learned one rule at a time. Even though readers can recognize good writing, researchers have not succeeding in completely describing just what it is that makes a "good" writing style good. It is, therefore, sensible to suppose that writing style is not consciously learned but is largely absorbed, or subconsciously acquired, from reading.

□ *Formal language is too complex to be learned one rule at a time.*

According to common wisdom, we learn to write by actually writing. The reading hypothesis asserts that this is not true, at least as far as style is concerned. Smith (1988) tells us why we do not learn to write by writing:

> I thought the answer [to how we learn to write] must be that we learn to write by writing until I reflected on how little anyone writes in school, even the eager students, and how little feedback is provided .... No one writes enough to learn more than a small part of what writers need to know. (p. 19)

The research confirms Smith's reflections.

□ *We do not learn to write by writing.*

Actual writing in school appears to be infrequent. Here is one typical report: Applebee, Langer, and Mullis (1986) asked students how many essays and reports they had written over six weeks for any school subject. Only 18.6 percent of the fourth graders wrote more than 10, while only 7.8 percent of the eleventh graders wrote more than 10.

□ *The actual amount of writing done by a typical student is low.*

Writing outside of school is also not frequent: Applebee et al.'s 11th graders did the most out-of-school writing, but only 17.4 percent kept diaries, 37.3 percent said that they wrote letters to friends, and 74.8 percent said they wrote notes and messages at least weekly. (See also Applebee et al. 1990 and Snow, Barnes, Chandler, Goodman, and Hemphill 1991 for similar results.)

Research by Rice (1986) allows us to make at least a crude comparison of writing and reading frequency outside of school. Rice probed reading and writing behavior of several groups, and I present one of them (high verbal adults) as a representative sample. These subjects reported 15.1 hours per week in "total reading," but only two hours per week in writing (1.9 hours for "short writing" and .1 hour for "long writing"). Assuming even a very slow reading rate (200 words per minute) and a very fast writing rate (typing at 60 words per minute), this still means that people deal with far more words in reading than in writing, a ratio of 25 to 1. More likely, the true ratio is closer to 150 to 1. Considering the complexity of the system that is to be acquired, these data severely weaken the case for writing as an important source of language acquisition. (See also Evans and Gleadow 1983 for similar estimates of reading and writing frequency. Thanks to e-mail, people may be writing more these days. This possibility has not been investigated to my knowledge.)

□ *People encounter far more language in reading than in writing.*

More Writing Does Not Mean Better Writing

Several additional reports have confirmed that students do little writing in school and outside of school: The recently published National Council on Writing report (2003) noted that according to the NAEP data, students in elementary school spend on the average only three hours per week or less on writing assignments. They recommend that schools double the amount of time students spend writing, and insist that "writing be taught in all subjects and at all grade levels" (p. 3). The research, however, does not support this simple solution: More writing does not necessarily lead to better writing.

Although some studies show that good writers do more writing than poor writers (see Applebee et al. 1990 and studies summarized in Krashen 1984), increasing the amount of writing students do does not increase their writing proficiency. First language studies in English include Dressel, Schmid, and Kincaid (1952); Arnold (1964); and Varble (1990). First language studies showing no relationship between writing frequency and quality in Chinese are Lee and Krashen (1997) and Lee (2001). Hunting (1967) describes unpublished dissertation research showing that writing quantity is not related to writing quality. An exception is Lokke and Wykoff (1948); very small differences were found, however, between college freshmen who wrote two themes per week and those who wrote one theme a week. In addition, Hillocks (1986), after an extensive review that included unpublished dissertation research, found that writing classes that emphasized free writing did not produce significantly better writing than comparison classes.

□ *Numerous studies show that increasing writing quantity does not affect writing quality.*

Second language studies include Burger (1989) and Mason (2003). Burger's subjects were students of English as a second language in Ottawa, Canada, enrolled in sheltered subject matter courses (teaching language through content). She reported that adding an extra class on writing, which included correction of students' written errors, had no impact on writing quality or on tests of general English proficiency.

Mason (2003), in a study of adult (college student) EFL in Japan, compared the effect of three different activities as a supplement to free voluntary reading: writing short commentaries of what was read in the first language (Japanese), writing commentaries in the second language (English), and writing commentaries in the second language and getting errors corrected. She found no difference among the three groups in gains in writing accuracy (or reading achievement) after three semesters. In addition, the extra time devoted to writing clearly made no contribution to language development: The two groups who wrote in English devoted an extra two hours per week to writing in English, with no dividends in increased proficiency.

□ *Language acquisition comes from input, not output; from comprehension, not production.*

Hypothesizing that writing style comes from reading, not writing, is consistent with what is known about language acquisition: Language acquisition comes from input, not output, from comprehension, not production. Thus, if you write a page a day, your writing style or your command of mechanics will not improve. However, other good things may result from your writing, as we shall see in the next section.

No studies, to my knowledge, have attempted to find a relationship between what is read and writing style. Such a relationship surely exists, because different styles have different linguistic characteristics. Smith (1988) has noted this, and advises: "To learn to write for newspapers, you must read newspapers; textbooks about them will not suffice. For magazines, browse through magazines rather than through correspondence courses on magazine writing. To write poetry, read it" (p. 20).

Nevertheless, it is probably true that reading anything at all will help all writing, at least to some extent. Although there are clearly different styles of prose, there is also considerable overlap among styles (Biber 1986): So-called narrative style has, for example, some but not all of the characteristics of formal, expository prose. Thus, reading novels will not make you a competent essayist; you will have to read lots of essays to develop the essay-type style. But reading novels will provide at least some of the features of essay style; a novel reader will write a much better essay, stylistically, than someone who has read little of anything. And, as emphasized throughout this book, doing light reading will provide the competence that makes heavier reading more comprehensible.

What Writing Does

Although writing does not help us develop writing style, writing has other virtues. As Smith (1988) has pointed out, we write for at least two reasons. First, and most obvious, we write to communicate with others. But perhaps more important, we write for ourselves, to clarify and stimulate our thinking. Most of our writing, even if we are published authors, is for ourselves.

As Elbow (1973) has noted, it is difficult to hold more than one thought in mind at a time. When we write our ideas down, the vague and abstract become clear and concrete. When thoughts are on paper, we can see the relationships among them, and can come up with better thoughts. Writing, in other words, can make you smarter.

□ *Writing can help us think through and solve problems.*

Readers who keep a diary or journal know all about this—you have a problem, you write it down, and at least some of the problem disappears. Sometimes the entire problem goes away.

Here is an example of this happening, a letter written to Ann Landers in 1976:

> Dear Ann: I'm a 26-year-old woman and feel like a fool asking you this question, but—should I marry the guy or not? Jerry is 30, but sometimes he acts like 14 . . .
>
> Jerry is a salesman and makes good money but has lost his wallet three times since I've known him and I've had to help him meet the payments on his car.
>
> The thing that bothers me most, I think, is that I have the feeling he doesn't trust me. After every date he telephones. He says it's to "say an extra goodnight," but I'm sure he is checking to see if I had a late date with someone else.
>
> One night I was in the shower and didn't hear the phone. He came over and sat on the porch all night. I found him asleep on the swing when I went to get the paper the next morning at 6:30 A.M. I had a hard time convincing him I had been in the house the whole time.
>
> Now on the plus side: Jerry is very good-looking and appeals to me physically. Well—that does it. I have been sitting here with this pen in my hand for 15 minutes trying to think of something else good to say about him and nothing comes to mind.
>
> Don't bother to answer this. You have helped me more than you will ever know.—Eyes Opened. (Permission granted by Ann Landers and Creators Syndicate.)

Perhaps the clearest experimental evidence showing that writing helps thinking is from a series of studies by Langer and Applebee (1987). High school students were asked to read social studies passages and then study the information in them either by writing an analytic essay on an assigned question relating to the passage, or by using other study techniques (e.g., note taking, answering comprehension questions, writing summaries, "normal" studying without writing). Students were then given a variety of tests on the material in the passages. Langer and Applebee reported that "in general, any kind of written response leads to better performance than does reading without writing" (p. 130). In their third study, they showed that essay writing did not result in greater retention when the reading passage was easy; when the passage they read was difficult, however, essay writers did much better than students using other study techniques. Similar results have been reported by Newell (1984), Marshall (1987), and Newell and Winograd (1989).

☐ *Studies show that writing can help thinking.*

Sometimes just a little bit of writing can make a big difference. In Ganguli's study (1989) college mathematics students who devoted three minutes per period to describing in writing an important concept covered in class easily outperformed a comparison group on the semester final exam. For a review of additional research supporting the hypothesis that writing "can make you smarter," see Applebee (1984), Boice (1994), and Krashen (2003a).[3]

The Effect of Television

It is widely assumed that watching television has a negative effect on reading and other aspects of language. There are at least two commonsense arguments against television. First, watching TV takes time, time that could be spent reading (this is known as the "displacement argument"). The evidence, we will see, is not clear.

☐ *It is widely assumed that television has a negative effect on reading. Not so.*

A second argument against television is that TV programs do not provide the kind of input that would stimulate language development. According to the research, this assertion is true: TV language is not nearly as complex as book language. Nevertheless, a moderate amount of TV watching appears to be harmless; studies show no significant impact of TV watching on tests of literacy and school performance, unless the amount of TV watching is excessive.

Does More Television Mean Less Reading?

The view that television watching displaces reading is a popular one, and a few case histories appear to support it. Some of the college students in Carlsen and Sherrill (1988) blamed television for preventing them from becoming readers and, in the following case, for extinguishing their interest in reading: "I continued this avid interest in reading until I was in the fifth grade. Then the one-eyed monster, commonly known as television, entered the realms of our living room. . . . To say the least, the television set replaced any book" (p. 138).

Some empirical studies appear to support this observation: In a study of sixth graders, Medrich, Roizen, Rubin and Buckley (1982) reported that high-volume TV watchers were less likely to be regular recreational readers than those who were moderate watchers, who in turn read less than those who were low-volume watchers. Amount of TV watching, however, is related to socioeconomic class, with lower-income families watching significantly more television (research reviewed in Comstock and Paik 1991). As we have seen, those in lower-income families have far less access to books. Thus, the correlation between TV watching and book reading may be spurious, a result of the fact that those in poorer families watch more TV and have less access to books. Access to books could be the actual cause of less frequent reading, not more TV. This interpretation is consistent with other studies showing no relationship between TV watching and reading, reviewed below.

When television is new, it can displace reading. This effect occurs when TV is initially introduced into a community (Brown, Cramond, and Wilde 1974) and when viewers are very young (preschoolers in Burton, Calonico, and McSeveney 1979; six-year-olds in Gadberry 1980). Some early studies done when television was just introduced in the United States also showed that TV watchers read less (Coffin 1948; Maccoby 1951) as did a survey carried out in 1965–1966 of the impact of TV in 14 countries (Robinson 1972).

☐ *When television is new, it can displace reading. When it is more established, it does not.*

When television is more established in a community, TV viewers read just as much as nonviewers, however (Himmelweit, Oppenheim, and Vince 1958), and subsequent studies done in the United States show no relationship between television watching and book reading (Schramm, Lyle, and Parker 1961; Robinson 1980; Zuckerman, Singer, and Singer 1980; but see McEvoy and Vincent 1980, who found no difference in TV watching between "light" and "heavy" readers but reported that "nonreaders" watched more television). Robinson and Godbey (1997) reported an increase in TV watching from 1965 to 1985 in the United States but also reported a slight increase in time spent reading books and magazines; newspaper reading, however, declined during this time.[4]

In an ethnographic study of three families, Neuman (1995) concluded that TV watching was much less likely to displace storybook reading to children when storybook time was "a structured family activity" (p. 168), taking place regularly at a specific time. TV watching, she noted, was often a default activity, taking place "because it happens to be there when other, even possibly more attractive, activities are not" (p. 170).

Some studies suggest that television can actually encourage reading: The dramatization of a book on television increases the likelihood that the book will be read (Himmelweit, Oppenheim, and Vince 1958; Busch 1978; Wendelin and Zinck 1983; Campbell, Griswald, and Smith 1988). The Book Industry Study Group (1984, cited in Neuman 1995, p. 103) reported, however, than only 4 percent of children they studied chose a book on the basis of seeing or hearing about it on television. It is also possible that television does not increase all reading, but "redirects the existing reading choice of an audience" (Beentjes and Van der Voort 1988, p. 392).

It has also been argued that television discourages reading and other uses of literacy because television characters are rarely seen reading or writing, or even behaving as if they read and write. As Postman (1983) has pointed out:

> It is quite noticeable that the majority of adults on TV shows are depicted as functionally illiterate, not only in the sense that the content of book learning is absent from what they appear to know but also because of the absence of even the faintest signs of a contemplative habit of mind. (p. 12)

The Language of Television

☐ *Television does not provide high-quality linguistic input.*

There is some basis for the second accusation presented at the beginning of this section: Television does not provide high-quality linguistic input.

Fasick (1973) reported that the language used in children's books was significantly more complicated than the language used in children's television shows. For example, 64 percent of the sentences in books (five books recommended for reading aloud to preschool children) were "complex," compared to 34 percent for television ("Captain Kangaroo" and two cartoons). Moreover, the complex sentences found in books involved more subordination. In other words, the complex sentences of the books were more complex. Fasick concluded that the language of television was only about as complicated as the speech of average fifth graders.

□ *The language of children's books is more complex than that of children's television.*

Liberman (1979) analyzed the language used in programs popular in the 1970s. His analysis of sentence complexity is in close agreement with Fasick's results. In addition, Liberman also reported that the quantity of language used on television was low. Of the eight shows Liberman analyzed, the one using the largest number of words, *M.A.S.H.*, contained a total of 3,395 words, and only 900 different words.

□ *The quantity of language used on television is low.*

Liberman concluded that "very likely, the lexicon of TV programming is under 5,000 words" (1979, p. 604), a pathetic result when one considers that estimates of first graders' vocabulary size range from 5,500 to 32,000 words (Smith 1941). Liberman's conclusions are supported by Hayes and Ahrens (1988), a study we discussed in chapter 2. Recall that Hayes and Ahrens found that the language of TV and ordinary conversation, whether between adults and adults or adults and children, was similar in terms of vocabulary. For all three, about 95 percent of the words used were from the most frequent 5,000 words in English. Printed texts, including comic books, children's books, and magazines, contained far more uncommon words.

Television shows may provide some input of value for young children in early stages of language acquisition (Rice and Haight 1986). They do not, however, compare very well to reading, either in terms of the complexity or the amount of language they provide.

Television and Language
Development

The impact of television on school-related measures, including reading comprehension, vocabulary, spelling, and "language arts," has been thoroughly studied. Several careful reviews of this research have been done (Williams, Haertel, Haertel, and Walberg 1982; Beentjes and Van der Voort 1988; Comstock and Paik 1991; Neuman 1995; see also studies by Neuman 1988 and Foertsch 1992), and they arrive at similar conclusions:

☐ *The impact of TV on reading is negative only when TV watching is excessive.*

- The overall impact of television is negative, but slight. In fact, it is hardly detectable. No matter what measures of achievement are examined, more television watching means only slightly reduced performance in reading comprehension, vocabulary, and other school-related measures.

- Several studies find that achievement actually increases (slightly) with moderate amounts of TV watching; that is, the more TV, the better watchers do on school-related tests. The relationship holds only up to about two hours of TV per day. After reaching this threshold, the relationship is negative: The more TV, the worse watchers do, with TV watching showing a clearly negative impact when it exceeds four hours per day (see, e.g., Neuman 1988, 1995). Interestingly, increased television watching is associated with better literacy development for children acquiring English as a second language (Blosser 1988); this relationship did not hold true for beginners, however, for whom English-language television was probably not comprehensible.

• There is some evidence that television has more negative effects on older students (high school; Neuman 1988) and on those in higher socioeconomic classes (Beentjes and Van der Voort 1988), but the impact remains small. Also, as one would expect, there is evidence that the impact of television depends on what programs children watch, with lower achievement related to watching entertainment-type and adventure programs (Neuman 1988).[5]

In general, however, correlations between what is watched and reading achievement are very modest (Degrotsky 1981; Potter 1987); the only substantial correlation reported by Potter (1987) was a negative relationship between watching soap operas and knowledge of science. Jönsson (1986), however, reported that preschool children whose parents "helped them to assimilate and understand television messages and kept a check on their televiewing" (p. 32) did better in school later on, and fifth graders who watched more documentaries did better in grade six.

☐ *Television is not the culprit in the "literacy crisis." The culprit is the absence of reading material.*

Television: A Summary

Much of what is on television may not be of high quality; nevertheless, television is clearly not the culprit in the "literacy crisis." Although the language of many TV shows is not impressive,

145

there is no clear evidence that TV displaces reading, and there is only a weak negative relationship between TV watching and performance on school-related tests. In fact, a little TV watching appears to be better than none at all, and TV watching may be helpful for second language acquisition. It is only when television watching is excessive that a clear negative effect appears, what Trelease (2001) refers to as "over-viewing" of TV.

Phrased slightly differently, it seems that those who do better on tests of language and literacy read more, but watch TV only a little less. Apparently it is not the presence of television that prevents children from reading; more likely, it is the absence of interesting books. Corteen and Williams (1986) agree: Consistent with the results of other studies, they found a negative correlation between amount of TV watching and reading achievement, but the size of the relationship was small, and they conclude that "the absence of reading practice is, in our view, more important than television" (p. 71).[6]

A final bit of data confirms this conclusion. Neuman (1995) compared the book choices of children who were heavy readers and heavy TV watchers, heavy readers and light TV watchers, and light readers and heavy TV watchers. The first two groups chose books of equally high quality (according to a scale measuring intellectual challenge, complexity, and richness of ideas), and both groups of heavy readers chose books of higher quality than the light readers. TV watching does not displace reading, nor does it mean lower-quality reading.

Second Language Acquirers

When second language acquirers read for pleasure, they develop the competence to move from the beginning "ordinary conversational" level to a level where they can use the second language for more demanding purposes, such as the study of literature, business, and so on. As some of the studies discussed earlier in this volume show, when second language acquirers read for pleasure, they can continue to improve in their second language without classes, without teachers, without study, and even without people to converse with (e.g., Cho's Sweet Valley studies, discussed in chapter 2).

There are also compelling reasons for encouraging recreational reading in the first language for second language acquirers. In early stages, it can profoundly accelerate the development of reading ability in the second language.

□ *Pleasure reading allows second language acquirers to improve without going to class.*

First, if it is true that we "learn to read by reading" (Goodman 1982; Smith 1994b), it is obviously easier to learn to read in a language the reader understands. Thus, it will be easier to learn to read in the primary language. Once the ability to read is acquired, there is good evidence that much of this ability transfers to the second language, even when the writing systems are different (Cummins 1981). There is strong correlational evidence supporting this hypothesis, as well as compelling case histories (Krashen 2003c).

□ *Learning to read in the first language is a short cut to second language reading.*

Second, as discussed in chapter 1, reading provides knowledge, knowledge of the world as well as subject matter knowledge. The knowledge gained through the first language can make second language input much more comprehensible.

Third, there is reason to suspect that the pleasure reading habit itself transfers. A pleasure reader in the first language will become a pleasure reader in the second language (Camiciottoli 2001).

Evidence confirming that reading in the first language is helpful for second language acquisition comes from the documented success of bilingual programs that provide literacy development and subject matter teaching in the primary language. Such programs, it has been shown, teach English as well as or better than programs in which children are taught in English all day (for reviews, see Willig 1985; Greene 1997. An especially complete recent study is Oller and Eilers 2002).

Recreational reading can also be of tremendous help for those who wish to continue to develop their primary or "heritage" language (HL). Contrary to popular opinion, it is very difficult to continue to develop one's primary language while living in another country. The most obvious barrier is lack of input; if one only uses the heritage language at home, there are of course limits to how far one can develop the language. Other barriers are less obvious, but are powerful: There is evidence that some heritage language speakers go through a stage of rejection or avoidance of the heritage culture (Tse 1998) and may avoid using the heritage language. Those in this stage of "ethnic ambivalence/evasion" will not improve their heritage language competence, regardless of whether input is available or not. Finally, some imperfect heritage language speakers report that their efforts to use the language are met with correction and even ridicule by more competent HL speakers, a reaction that discourages the use of the HL (Gupta and Yeok 1995; Krashen 1998b).

A big part of the solution for those lacking input or facing ridicule is a method that supplies input and works for shy people: recreational reading. Several studies confirm that recreational reading works for heritage language development: Tse (2001) reported that those who "beat the odds" and managed to maintain unusually high levels of competence in their heritage language had access to reading materials in the heritage language, and nearly all developed an interest in reading in the language for pleasure. Cho and Krashen (2000) found four independent predictors of HL competence among second-generation Korean HL speakers: parental use of the HL, trips to Korea, TV watching, and recreational reading. McQuillan (1998b) reported that Spanish classes at the university of level for native speakers of Spanish that emphasized pleasure reading and discussion of texts of interest resulted in more enthusiasm for Spanish reading as well as better gains in vocabulary, as compared to traditional instruction.

It is easy to say that recreational reading in the primary language can be a big help, but there is a major barrier that prevents implementation: little access to books. A huge percentage of limited English speaking children in the United States are Spanish-speakers. As noted in chapter 2, Spanish speaking limited English proficient children have very little access to books in Spanish, at home (Ramirez et al. 1991) or in school (Pucci 1994).[7]

□ *Few books are available in primary or heritage languages.*

Conclusions

My conclusions are simple. When children read for pleasure, when they get "hooked on books," they acquire, involuntarily and without conscious effort, nearly all of the so-called language skills many people are so concerned about: They will become adequate readers, acquire a large vocabulary, develop the ability to understand and use complex grammatical constructions, develop a good writing style, and become good (but not necessarily perfect) spellers. Although free voluntary reading alone will not ensure the attainment of the

□ *Children who are readers will develop at least acceptable levels of literacy. Without a reading habit, children simply do not have a chance.*

highest levels of literacy, it will at least ensure an acceptable level. It will also provide the competence necessary for dealing with demanding texts.[8] Without it, I suspect that children simply do not have a chance.

☐ *Well-read people write well because they have subconsciously acquired good writing style.*

When we read, we really have no choice—we must develop literacy. We rarely find well-read people who have serious problems with grammar, spelling, and so on. They write acceptably well because they can't help it; they have subconsciously acquired good writing style as well as all or nearly all of the conventions of writing.

☐ *FVR is not a replacement for the language program. FVR complements language arts classes.*

I am not, however, proposing a language arts program consisting only of free reading. I also recognize the value of reading that is assigned by teachers, and reading that is recommended by teachers, librarians, and parents. A language arts class, in my view, is primarily a literature class. Assigned reading and free voluntary reading will help each other: Through literature, students will grow intellectually and be exposed to a wider variety of books, which can stimulate more free reading. In fact, one of the ways we know that a literature program is effective is if it results in more free voluntary reading. In turn, free voluntary reading will help build language competence and contribute to intellectual growth, which will make literature more comprehensible and meaningful.

☐ *We have confused cause and effect.*

Our problem in language education, as Frank Smith has pointed out, is that we have confused cause and effect. We have assumed that we first master language "skills" and then apply these skills to reading and writing. But that is not the way the human brain operates. Rather, reading for meaning, reading about things that matter to us, is the cause of literate language development.

If this view is even partly correct, it means that we need to create a print-rich environment for children both inside and outside school. It means that teachers need to be assured that creating such an environment will make their jobs easier, not harder, and will give more satisfying results.

Administrators need to know that when teachers are reading to students, and when teachers are relaxing with a good book during sustained silent reading sessions, teachers are doing their job. Administrators need to know that a print-rich environment is not a luxury but a necessity. (Administrators will be relieved to know that creating a print-rich environment is not excessively expensive: For the price of a few computers, a school library can be significantly improved.) Administrators will also be pleased to know that providing a print-rich environment will lead to an easier and more productive day for teachers, with improved student competence in reading and language arts, competence that shows up in real life as well as on standardized test scores.

☐ *The true path to higher test scores is reading.*

Parents need to know that children will get far more benefit from being read to, from seeing parents read for pleasure, and from reading comics, graphic novels, magazines, and books, than they will from working through workbooks on sale at the local drug store.

☐ *Parents should opt for actual reading rather than using workbooks.*

Finally, there is no question that reading is pleasant; as we have seen, the research literature is replete with reports of the pleasure children get from free reading (see chapter 1, "The Pleasure of Reading" section), as well as the boredom that often accompanies some required reading and workbook exercises. While it may not be true that everything that is good for you is pleasant, the most effective way of building literacy happens to be the most pleasant.

Notes

1. The Smith-Goodman view of reading as the confirmation of predictions has been challenged. For discussion and a response to some critics, see Krashen (1999).

2. Smith's hypothesis explains why some of us cannot seem to write convincingly in certain styles, despite massive reading of texts written in these styles. I have read widely, but seem only to be able to write comfortably in the academic (or at best modified academic) style you are reading now, reflecting the club I have joined. (I have been told that even my personal letters read like journal papers.) Smith's hypothesis also explains, conversely, why reading just a modest amount of authors we admire can influence our writing style.

3. Strong confirmation that writing helps thinking is the work of Robert Boice. Boice (1983) concluded that regularly scheduled writing sessions encouraged more writing and the emergence of more creative ideas than did "spontaneous" writing (writing when the writer "felt like it"). Boice asked college students to write under several conditions: not to write at all for several weeks (control group), to write only when they felt like it, or to write regularly at scheduled sessions each day. Subjects were asked to keep track of the number of pages written and the number of creative or novel ideas they came up with. Regular daily writing resulted in about double the number of pages written and double the number of new ideas, as compared to writing when one felt like it. The control group reported the fewest number of new

ideas. Boice has recommended a modest amount of regular daily writing in several of his publications (see especially Boice 1994). There is no doubt in my mind that it works. I would never have completed this edition of this book without following Boice's suggestions.

4. There is some evidence supporting the reasonable hypothesis that what children watch is related to how much they read. In agreement with other research, Zuckerman, Singer, and Singer (1980) found no overall relationship between time spent watching TV and time spent reading, but they also found that children who watched more "fantasy violent" programs tended to read less. Schramm, Lyle, and Parker (1961) also reported no relation between TV watching and book reading, but found that children who watch more TV read fewer comic books (see also Murray and Kippax 1978 for similar results; Williams and Boyes 1986, however, found a slight positive correlation between TV watching and comic book reading).

5. This is consistent with research showing that children who watch more "violent fantasy" programs do less reading, as mentioned in note 4. Cleary (1939) found that the impact of radio in the 1930s was remarkably similar to the impact of television today. Cleary concluded that overall, "radio listening does not seriously restrict the amount or quality of reading" (p. 126). Although those who listened to the radio a great deal (more than three hours per day) read fewer books (but read more newspapers and magazines), those who did very little listening to the radio had less interest in reading. Cleary also reported that heavy moviegoers, those who attended more than three films per week (5 percent of her sample), read more books and read higher-quality books.

6. Computer use, contrary to popular opinion, appears to be mildly positively related to reading. Robinson and Godbey (1997) reported positive but small correlations between amount of computer use and time spent reading books for adults: More computer use was associated with more reading. The relationship remained significant even when the researchers controlled for social class; this is important to do because higher-income people are more likely to have computers and to read more. Of great interest is the finding that the relationship also held for different uses of the computer. Time spent word processing, using the computer for financial purposes, and playing games on the computer (!) all correlated positively with time spent reading. Time spent on the computer was negatively correlated with time spent watching TV, but again the relationship was small. The results of a recent Gallup Poll (Gallup 2002) confirmed that computers do not bleed reading time: Those who regularly use computers spend as much time reading as those who do not.

7. Pucci and Ulanoff (1996) surveyed 32 school librarians: 54 percent said that books written in Spanish were difficult to obtain, and 70 percent said that their cost was "prohibitive." Of 5,000 books on one approved reading list for purchase for school libraries, only 300 were in Spanish. Pucci and Ulanoff note that "even if these books were age appropriate, a child reading two books per week would finish every Spanish volume in the library before entering fourth grade" (p. 114).

8. As noted in chapter 2, note 6, there are clear differences between different genres. But there is overlap: Reading in any genre will help make any other genre more comprehensible. A student about to take ninth-grade world history who has read 100 Sweet Valley High novels will have more success

with the history texts than a classmate who has done little or no recreational reading. And one who has read all the Harry Potter novels (five have been published at the time of this writing) will probably have very few problems.

References

Alexander, F. 1986. *California assessment program: Annual report.* Sacramento: California State Department of Education.

Allen, L., J. Cipielewski, and K. Stanovich. 1992. Multiple indicators of children's reading habits and attitudes: Construct validity and cognitive correlates. *Journal of Educational Psychology* 84: 489–503.

Allington, R. 1980. Poor readers don't get to read much in reading groups. *Language Arts* 57: 872–876.

Allington, R., S. Guice, K. Baker, N. Michaelson, and S. Li. 1995. Access to books: Variations in schools and classrooms. *The Language and Literacy Spectrum* 5: 23–25.

Anderson, R., P. Wilson, and L. Fielding. 1988. Growth in reading and how children spend their time outside of school. *Reading Research Quarterly* 23: 285–303.

Applebee, A. 1978. Teaching high-achievement students: A survey of the winners of the 1977 NCTE Achievement Awards in writing. *Research in the Teaching of English* 1: 41–53.

———. 1984. Writing and reasoning. *Review of Educational Research* 54: 577–596.

Applebee, A., J. Langer, and I. Mullis. 1986. *The writing report card.* Princeton, N.J.: Educational Testing Service.

Applebee, A., J. Langer, I. Mullis, L. Jenkins, and M. Foertsch. 1990. *Learning to write in our nation's schools: Instruction and achievement in 1988 at grades 4, 8, and 12.* Princeton, N.J.: Educational Testing Service.

Appleby, B., and J. Conner. 1965. Well, what did you think of it? *English Journal* 54: 606–612.

Aranha, M. 1985. Sustained silent reading goes east. *Reading Teacher* 39: 214–217.

Aranow, M. 1961. A study of the effect of individualized reading on children's reading test scores. *Reading Teacher* 15: 86–91.

Arlin, M., and G. Roth. 1978. Pupil's use of time while reading comics and books. *American Educational Research Journal* 5: 201–216.

Arnold, L. 1964. Writer's cramp and eyestrain—are they paying off? *English Journal* 53: 10–15.

Asimov, I. 2002. *It's been a good life.* New York: Prometheus Books.

Bader, L., J. Veatch, and J. Eldridge. 1987. Trade books or basal readers? *Reading Improvement* 24: 62–67.

Bailey, A. 1969. How parents feel about individualized reading. In *Individualized reading: Readings,* ed. S. Duker. Metuchen, N.J.: Scarecrow, pp. 325–330.

Bailyn, L. 1959. Mass media and children: A study of exposure habits and cognitive effects. *Psychological Monographs* 73: 201–216.

Baughman, J. 2000. *School libraries and MCAS scores.* Available: http://artemis. simmons.edu/~baughman/mcas-school-libraries.

Beck, I., M. McKeown, and E. McCaslin. 1983. Vocabulary development: Not all contexts are created equal. *Elementary School Journal* 83: 177–181.

Beentjes, J., and T. Van der Voort. 1988. Television's impact on children's reading skills: A review of the research. *Psychological Monographs* 73: 201–216.

Biber, D. 1986. Spoken and written textual dimensions in English. *Language* 62: 384–414.

Bintz, W. 1993. Resistant readers in secondary education: Some insights and implications. *Journal of Reading* 36(8): 604–615.

Blakely, W. 1958. A study of seventh grade children's reading of comic books as related to certain other variables. *Journal of Genetic Psychology* 93: 291–301.

Blok, H. 1999. Reading to young children in educational settings: A meta-analysis of recent research. *Language Learning* 49 (2): 343–371.

Blosser, B. 1988. Television, reading and oral language development: The case of the Hispanic child. *NABE Journal* 13: 21–42.

Bohnhorst, B., and S. Sellars. 1959. Individual reading instruction vs. basal textbook instruction: Some tentative explorations. *Elementary English* 36: 185–202.

Boice, R. 1983. Contingency management in writing and the appearance of creative ideas: Implications for the treatment of writing blocks. *Behavioral Research Therapy* 21 (5): 537–43.

———. 1994. *How writers journey to comfort and fluency.* Westport, Conn.: Praeger.

Brandenburg, G. 1919. Some possibly secondary factors in spelling ability. *School and Society* 9: 632–636.

Brassell, D. 2003. Sixteen books went home tonight: Fifteen were introduced by the teacher. *The California Reader* 36 (3): 33–39.

Brazerman, C. 1985. Physicists reading physics: Schema-laden purposes and purpose-laden schema. *Written Communication* 2: 3–43.

Brocka, B. 1979. Comic books: In case you haven't noticed, they've changed. *Media and Methods* 15: 30–32.

Brown, J., J. Cramond, and R. Wilde. 1974. Displacement effects of television and the child's functional orientation to media. In *Children's understanding of television,* ed. J. Bryant and D. Anderson. New York: Academic Press, pp. 1–33.

Burger, S. 1989. Content-based ESL in a sheltered psychology course: Input, output, and outcomes. *TESL Canada* 6: 45–59.

Burley, J. 1980. Short-term, high intensity reading practice methods for upward bound students: An appraisal. *Negro Educational Review* 31(3–4): 156–161.

Burton, S., J. Calonico, and D. McSeveney. 1979. Effects of preschool television watching on first-grade children. *Journal of Communication* 29(3): 164–170.

Bus, A., M. Van Ijzendoorn, and A. Pellegrini. 1995. Joint book reading makes for success in learning to read: A meta-analysis on intergenerational transmission of literacy. *Review of Educational Research* 65: 1–21.

Busch, J. 1978. Television's effects on reading: A case study. *Phi Beta Kappan* 59: 668–671.

Business Week Online. 2002. *Comics clamber back from the brink.* Available: http://businessweek.com/bwdaily/dnflash/aug2002/nf20020829_ 2344.htm.

Bustead, A. 1943. Finding the best method for memorizing. *The Journal of Educational Psychology* 34: 110–114.

Camiciottoli, B. C. 2001. Extensive reading in English: Habits and attitudes of a group of Italian university students. *Journal of Research in Reading* 24(2): 135–153.

Campbell, C., D. Griswald, and F. H. Smith. 1988. Effects of tradebook covers (hardback or paperback) on individualized reading choices by elementary-age children. *Reading Improvement* 25: 166–178.

Campbell, D., and J. Stanley. 1966. *Experimental and quasi-experimental designs for research.* Chicago: Rand McNally.

Carlsen, G. R., and A. Sherrill. 1988. *Voices of readers: How we come to love books.* Urbana, Ill.: NCTE.

Carson, B. 1990. *Gifted hands.* Grand Rapids, Mich.: Zondervan Books.

Carter, C. 1988. Does your child love to read? *Parade Magazine,* April 3.

Cho, G., and S. Krashen. 2000. The role of voluntary factors in heritage language development: How speakers can develop the heritage language on their own. ITL: *Review of Applied Linguistics* 127–128: 127–140.

Cho, K. S., and S. Krashen. 1994. Acquisition of vocabulary from the Sweet Valley High Kids series: Adult ESL acquisition. *Journal of Reading* 37: 662–667.

———. 1995a. From Sweet Valley Kids to Harlequins in one year. *California English* 1(1): 18–19.

———. 1995b. Becoming a dragon: Progress in English as a second language through narrow free voluntary reading. *California Reader* 29: 9–10.

———. 2002. Sustained silent reading experiences among Korean teachers of English as a foreign language: The effect of a single exposure to interesting, comprehensible reading. *Reading Improvement* 38(4): 170–174.

Chomsky, N. 1965. *Aspects of the theory of syntax.* Cambridge, Mass.: MIT Press.

Cipielewski, J., and K. Stanovich. 1990. Assessing print exposure and orthographic processing skill in children: a quick measure of reading experience. *Journal of Educational Psychology* 82: 733–740.

Cleary, F. 1939. Why children read. *Wilson Library Bulletin* 14: 119–126.

Cline, R., and G. Kretke. 1980. An evaluation of long-term SSR in the junior high school. *Journal of Reading* (March): 503–506.

Cline, Z., and J. Necochea. 2003. My mother never read to me. *Journal of Adolescent and Adult Literacy* 47 (2): 122–126.

Cocks, J. 1988. The passing of Pow! and Blam! Comics grow up, get ambitious, and turn into graphic novels. *Time Magazine,* January 25.

Coffin, T. 1948. Television's effect on leisure-time activities. *Journal of Applied Psychology* 32: 550–558.

Cohen, K. 1999. Reluctant eighth grade readers enjoy sustained silent reading. *California Reader* 33(1): 22–25.

Cohen, Y. 1997. How reading got me into trouble. Class paper, Trenton State University, Summer.

Coles, G. 2003. *Reading the naked truth: Literacy, legislation, and lies.* Portsmouth, N.H.: Heinemann.

Collins, C. 1980. Sustained silent reading periods: Effects of teachers' behaviors and students' achievements. *Elementary School Journal* 81: 109–114.

Comstock, G., and H. Paik. 1991. *Television and the American child.* New York: Academic Press.

Constantino, R. 1994. Immigrant ESL high school students' understanding and use of the school and public library. *SCOPE Journal* 93: 6–18.

———. Minority use of the library. *California Reader* 28: 10–12.

Constantino, R., S. Y. Lee, K. S. Cho, and S. Krashen. 1997. Free voluntary reading as a predictor of TOEFL scores. *Applied Language Learning* 8: 111–118.

Cook, W. 1912. Shall we teach spelling by rule? *Journal of Educational Psychology* 3: 316–325.

Cornman, O. 1902. *Spelling in the elementary school.* Boston: Ginn.

Corteen, R., and T. Williams. 1986. Television and reading skills. In *The impact of television*, ed. T. M. Williams. New York: Academic Press, pp. 39–86.

Csikszentmihalyi , M. 1991. *Flow: The psychology of optimal experience.* New York: HarperPerennial.

Cummins, J. 1981. The role of primary language development in promoting educational success for language minority students. In *Schooling and language minority students.* Sacramento: California Department of Education, pp. 3–49.

———. 1996. *Negotiating identities: Education for empowerment in a diverse society.* Los Angeles: California Association for Bilingual Education.

Cunningham, A., and K. Stanovich. 1990. Assessing print exposure and orthographic processing skill in children: A quick measure of reading experience. *Journal of Educational Psychology* 82: 733–740.

Curtiss, H., and E. Dolch. 1939. Do spelling books teach spelling? *Elementary School Journal* 39: 584–592.

Cyrog, F. 1962. Self-selection in reading: Report of a longitudinal study. In *Claremont reading conference: 26th yearbook,* ed. M. Douglas. Claremont, Calif.: Claremont Graduate School, pp. 106–113.

Daly, J., and D. Wilson. 1983. Writing apprehension, self-esteem, and personality. *Research in the Teaching of English* 17: 327–341.

Davis, F., and J. Lucas. 1971. An experiment in individualized reading. *Reading Teacher* 24: 737–743, 747.

Davis, Z. 1998. A comparison of the effectiveness of sustained silent reading and directed reading activity on students' reading achievement. *The High School Journal* 72(1): 46–48.

Day, R., C. Omura, and M. Hiramatsu. 1991. Incidental EFL vocabulary learning and reading. *Reading in a Foreign Language* 7(2): 541–551.

Degrotsky, D. 1981. *Television viewing and reading achievement of seventh and eighth graders.* ERIC Document No. ED 215 291.

Denton, K., and J. West. 2002. *Children's reading and mathematics achievement in kindergarten and first grade.* Washington, D.C.: National Center for Educational Statistics.

Di Loreto, C., and L. Tse. 1999. Seeing is believing: Disparity in books in two Los Angeles area public libraries. *School Library Quarterly* 17(3): 31–36.

Dirda, M. 2003. *An open book.* New York: Norton.

Doig, D., and A. Blackmore. 1995. Leisure reading: Attitudes and practices of Australian year 6 children. *Australian Journal of Language and Literacy* 18(3): 204–217.

Dorrell, L., and E. Carroll. 1981. Spider-Man at the library. *School Library Journal* 27: 17–19.

Dressell, P., J. Schmid, and G. Kincaid. 1952. The effects of writing frequency upon essay-type writing proficiency at the college level. *Journal of Educational Research* 46: 285–293.

Duggins, J. 1976. The elementary self-contained classroom. In *The new hooked on books,* ed. D. Fader. New York: Berkeley Books, pp. 181–190.

Duin, J. 2002. Comics still flying high. *The Washington Times,* February 6.

Duke, N. 2000. For the rich it's richer: Print experiences and environments offered to children in very low- and very high-socioeconomic status first-grade classrooms. *American Educational Research Journal* 37(2): 441–478.

Dulay, H., and M. Burt. 1977. Remarks on creativity in second language acquisition. In *Viewpoints on English as a second language,* ed. M. Burt, H. Dulay, and M. Finnocchiaro. New York: Regents, pp. 95–126.

Dulay, H., M. Burt, and S. Krashen. 1982. *Language two.* New York: Oxford University Press.

Dupuy, B. 1997. Voices from the classroom: Students favor extensive reading over grammar instruction and practice, and give their reasons. *Applied Language Learning* 8(2): 253–261.

———. 1998. Cercles de lecture: Une autre approche de la lecture dans la classe intermédiaire de français langue étrangrèe. *The Canadian Modern Language Review* 54 (4): 579–585.

Dupuy, B., and S. Krashen. 1993. Incidental vocabulary acquisition in French as a foreign language. *Applied Language Learning* 4 (1, 2): 55–63.

Elbow, P. 1973. *Writing without teachers.* New York: Oxford University Press.

Eller, R., C. Pappas, and E. Brown. 1988. The lexical development of kindergartners: Learning from written context. *Journal of Reading Behavior* 20: 5–24.

Elley, W. 1984. Exploring the reading difficulties of second language learners in Fiji. In *Reading in a second language,* ed. J. C. Alderson and A. Urquart. New York: Longman, pp. 281–301.

———. 1989. Vocabulary acquisition from listening to stories. *Reading Research Quarterly* 24: 174–187.

———. 1991. Acquiring literacy in a second language: The effect of book-based programs. *Language Learning* 41: 375–411.

———. 1992. *How in the world do students read?* Hamburg: The International Association for the Evaluation of Educational Achievement.

———. 1994. *IEA study of reading literacy.* Amsterdam: Elsevier Science.

———. 1998. *Raising literacy levels in third world countries: A method that works.* Culver City, Calif.: Language Education Associates.

Elley, W., I. Barham, H. Lamb, and M. Wyllie. 1976. The role of grammar in a secondary school curriculum. *Research in the Teaching of English* 10: 5–21.

Elley, W., and F. Mangubhai. 1983. The impact of reading on second language learning. *Reading Research Quarterly* 19: 53–67.

El-Shabbaz, E. 1964. *The autobiography of Malcolm X.* New York: Ballantine.

Emery, C., and M. Csikszentmihalyi. 1982. The socialization effects of cultural role models in ontogenetic development and upward mobility. *Child Psychiatry and Human Development* 12: 3–19.

Evans, H., and J. Towner. 1975. Sustained silent reading: Does it increase skills? *Reading Teacher* 29: 155–156.

Evans, P., and N. Gleadow. 1983. Literacy: A study of literacy performance and leisure activities in Victoria, BC. *Reading Canada Lecture* 2: 3–16.

Facemire, N. 2000. *The effect of the accelerated reader on the reading comprehension of third graders.* ERIC Document No. ED 442 097

Fader, D. 1976. *The new hooked on books.* New York: Berkeley Books.

Fadiman, C. 1947. *Party of one: The selected writings of Clifton Fadiman.* Cleveland: World Publishing.

Fairbank, Maslin, Maullin and Associates. 1999. *California Statewide Poll, Job # 620–157.* Santa Monica, Calif.: California Opinion Research.

Farrell, E. 1982. SSR as the core of junior high school reading program. *The Reading Teacher* 36: 48–51.

Fasick, A. 1973. Television language and book language. *Elementary English* 50: 125–131.

Feitelson, D., B. Kita, and A. Goldstein, 1986. Effects of listening to series stories on first graders' comprehension and use of language. *Research in the Teaching of English* 20: 339–355.

Filback, R., and S. Krashen. 2002. The impact of reading the bible and studying the bible on biblical knowledge. *Knowledge Quest* 31(2): 50–51.

Finegan, E. 1999. *Language: Its structure and use.* 3d ed. New York: Harcourt Brace.

Flurkey, A., and J. Xu, eds. 2003. *On the revolution in reading: The selected writings of Kenneth S. Goodman.* Portsmouth, N.H.: Heinemann.

Foertsch, M. 1992. *Reading in and out of school.* Washington, D.C.: U.S. Department of Education.

Frebody, P., and R. Anderson. 1983. Effects of text comprehension of differing proportions and locations of difficult vocabulary. *Journal of Reading Behavior* 15: 19–39.

Gadberry, S. 1980. Effects of restricting first graders' TV-viewing on leisure time use, IQ change, and cognitive style. *Journal of Applied Developmental Psychology* 1: 45–57.

Gallup. 2002. Does reading still stack up? Gallup Poll News Service, September 3. Available: 2002. http://www.gallup.com.

Ganguli, A. 1989. Integrating writing in developmental mathematics. *College Teaching* 37: 140–142.

Garan, E. 2002. *Resisting reading mandates.* Portsmouth, N.H.: Heinemann.

Gaver, M. 1963. *Effectiveness of centralized library service in elementary schools.* New Brunswick, N.J.: Rutgers University Press.

Gilbert, L. 1934a. Effect of spelling on reading in the ninth grade. *School Review* 42: 197–204.

———. 1934b. Effect of reading on spelling in the secondary schools. *California Quarterly of Secondary Education* 9: 269–275.

———. 1935. Study of the effect of reading on spelling. *Journal of Educational Research* 28: 570–586.

Goertzel, M., V. Goertzel, and T. Goertzel, T. 1978. *Three hundred eminent personalities.* San Francisco: Jossey-Bass.

Goodman, G. 1999. *The Reading Renaissance/Accelerated Reader program. Pinal County school-to-work evaluation report.* ERIC Document No. ED 427 299

Goodman, K. 1982. Language, literacy, and learning. London: Routledge Kagan Paul.

Goodman, K., and Y. Goodman. 1982. Spelling ability of a self-taught reader. In *Language and literacy: The selected writings of Kenneth S. Goodman,* vol. 2., ed. F. Gollasch. London: Routledge, pp. 135–142.

Gordon, I., and C. Clark. 1961. An experiment in individualized reading. *Childhood Education* 38: 112–113.

Gorman, M. 2002. Thirty graphic novels you can't live without. *School Library Journal* 48(8): 42–44, 47.

Gradman, H., and E. Hanania. 1991. Language learning background factors and ESL proficiency. *Modern Language Journal* 75: 39–51.

Graves, M., G. Brunett, and W. Slater. 1982. The reading vocabularies of primary grade children from varying geographic and social backgrounds. In *New Inquiries in Reading Research and Instruction,* ed. J. Niles and C. Harris. Rochester, NY: National Reading Conference, pp. 99–104.

Gray, G. 1969. A survey of children's attitudes toward individualized reading. In *Individualized reading: Readings,* ed. S. Duker. Metuchen, N.J.: Scarecrow, pp. 330–332.

Greaney, V. 1970. A comparison of individualized and basal reader approaches to reading instruction. *Irish Journal of Education* 1: 19–29.

———. 1980. Factors related to the amount and type of leisure time reading. *Reading Research Quarterly* 15: 337–357.

Greaney, V., and M. Clarke. 1973. A longitudinal study of the effects of two reading methods on leisure-time reading habits. In *Reading: What of the future?* ed. D. Moyle. London: United Kingdom Reading Association, pp. 107–114.

Greaney, V., and M. Hegarty. 1987. Correlations of leisure time reading. *Journal of Research in Reading* 10:3–20.

Greene, J. 1997. A meta-analysis of the Rossell and Baker review of bilingual education research. *Bilingual Research Journal* 21 (2, 3): 103–122.

Gupta, A., and S. P. Yeok. 1995. Language shift in a Singapore family. *Journal of Multilingual and Multicultural Development* 16(4): 301–314.

Hafiz, F., and I. Tudor. 1990. Graded readers as an input medium in L2 learning. *System* 18(1): 31–42.

Hafner, L., B. Palmer, and S. Tullos. 1986. The differential reading interests of good and poor readers in the ninth grade. *Reading Improvement* 23: 39–42.

Haggan, M. 1991. Spelling errors in native Arabic-speaking English majors: A comparison between remedial students and fourth year students. *System* 19: 45–61.

Hammill, D., S. Larsen, and G. McNutt. 1977. The effect of spelling instruction: A preliminary study. *Elementary School Journal* 78: 67–72.

Hartl, B. 2003. Comic relief: Heroic efforts keep Parts Unknown afloat. *The Business Journal of the Greater Triad Area*, March 31.

Haugaard, K. 1973. Comic books: A conduit to culture? *Reading Teacher* 27: 54–55.

Hayes, D., and M. Ahrens. 1988. Vocabulary simplification for children: A special case of "motherese"? *Journal of Child Language* 15: 395–410.

Healy, A. 1963. Changing children's attitudes toward reading. *Elementary English* 40: 255–257, 279.

Heisler, F. 1947. A comparison of comic book and non-comic book readers of the elementary school. *Journal of Educational Research* 40: 458–464.

Herbert, S. 1987. SSR—What do students think? *Journal of Reading* 30(7): 651.

Herda, R., and F. Ramos. 2001. How consistently do students read during sustained silent reading? *California School Library Journal* 24(2): 29–31.

Herman, P., R. Anderson, P. D. Pearson, and W. Nagy. 1987. Incidental acquisition of word meanings from expositions with varied text features. *Reading Research Quarterly* 22: 263–284.

Hermann, F. 2003. Differential effects of reading and memorization of paired associates on vocabulary acquisition in adult learners of English as a second language. *TESL-EJ* 7(1): A-1. Available: http://www-writing.berkeley.edu/TESOL-EJ.

Heyns, B. 1978. *Summer learning and the effects of schooling.* New York: Academic Press.

Hillocks, G., Jr. 1986. *Research on written composition: New directions for teaching.* ED 265552. Urbana, Ill.: ERIC.

Himmelweit, H., A. Oppenheim, and P. Vince. 1958. *Television and the child.* New York: Oxford University Press.

Holt, S., and F. O'Tuel. 1989. The effect of sustained silent reading and writing on achievement and attitudes of seventh and eighth grade students reading two years below grade level. *Reading Improvement* 26: 290–297.

Horst, M., T. Cobb, and P. Meara. 1998. Beyond Clockwork Orange: Acquiring second language vocabulary through reading. *Reading in a Foreign Language* 11(2): 207–223.

Houle, R., and C. Montmarquette. 1984. An empirical analysis of loans by school libraries. *Alberta Journal of Educational Research* 30: 104–114.

Hoult, T. 1949. Comic books and juvenile delinquency. *Sociology and Social Research* 33: 279–284.

Hughes, J. 1966. The myth of the spelling list. *National Elementary Principal* 46: 53–54.

Hunting, R. 1967. Recent studies of writing frequency. *Research in the Teaching of English* 1: 29–40.

Huser, M. 1967. Reading and more reading. *Elementary English* 44: 378–382, 385.

Inge, M. T. 1985. *The American comic book.* Columbus: Ohio State University.

Ingham, J. 1981. *Books and reading development: The Bradford book flood experiment.* London: Heinemann Educational Books.

Ivey, G., and K. Broaddus. 2001. "Just plain reading": A survey of what makes students want to read in middle school classrooms. *Reading Research Quarterly* 36(4): 350–377.

Jacoby, L., and A. Hollingshead. 1990. Reading student essays may be hazardous to your spelling: Effects of reading incorrectly and correctly spelled words. *Canadian Journal of Psychology* 44: 345–358.

Janopoulos, M. 1986. The relationship of pleasure reading and second language writing proficiency. *TESOL Quarterly* 20: 763–768.

Jenkins, M. 1957. Self-selection in reading. *Reading Teacher* 11: 84–90.

Johnson, R. 1965. Individualized and basal primary reading programs. *Elementary English* 42: 902–904, 915.

Jönsson, A. 1986. TV: A threat or a complement to school? *Journal of Educational Television* 12(1): 29–38.

Kaplan, J., and E. Palhinda. 1981. Non-native speakers of English and their composition abilities: A review and analysis. In *Linguistics and literacy,* ed. W. Frawley. New York: Plenum Press, pp. 425–457.

Kim, H., and S. Krashen. 1998a. The author and magazine recognition tests as predictors of literacy development in Korean. *Perceptual and Motor Skills* 87: 1376–1378.

———. 1998b. The author recognition and magazine recognition tests, and free voluntary reading as predictors of vocabulary development in English as a foreign language for Korean high school students. *System* 26: 515–523.

Kim, J. 2003. Summer reading and the ethnic achievement gap. Paper presented at the American Educational Research Association, Chicago, April 21.

Kim, J., and S. Krashen, S. 2000. Another home run. *California English* 6(2): 25

Kitao, K., M. Yamamoto, S. K. Kitao, and H. Shimatani. 1990. Independent reading in English—use of graded readers in the library English as a second language corner. *Reading in a Foreign Language* 6(2): 383–395.

Konopak. B. 1988. Effects of inconsiderate vs. considerate text on secondary students' vocabulary learning. *Journal of Reading Behavior* 20: 25–41.

Krashen, S. 1982. *Principles and practice in second language acquisition.* New York: Prentice Hall.

———. 1984. *Writing: Research, theory and applications.* Beverly Hills: Laredo Publishing.

———. 1985a. *The input hypothesis: Issues and implications.* Beverly Hills: Laredo.

———. 1985b. *Inquiries and insights.* Menlo Park: Calif.: Alemany Press.

———. 1988. Do we learn to reading by reading? The relationship between free reading and reading ability. In *Linguistics in context: Connecting observation and understanding,* ed. D. Tannen. Norwood, N.J.: Ablex, pp. 269–298.

———. 1989. We acquire vocabulary and spelling by reading: Additional evidence for the Input Hypothesis. *Modern Language Journal* 73: 440–464.

———. 1994. The pleasure hypothesis. In *Georgetown University Round Table on Languages and Linguistics,* ed. J. Alatis. Washington, D.C.: Georgetown University Press, pp. 299–302.

———. 1995. School libraries, public libraries, and the NAEP reading scores. *School Library Media Quarterly* 23: 235–238.

———. 1996. *Under attack: The case against bilingual education.* San Francisco: Alta Publishing.

———. 1998a. Why consider the library and books? In *Literacy, access, and libraries among the language minority population,* ed. R. Constantino. Lanham, Md.: Scarecrow, pp. 1–16.

———. 1998b. Language shyness and heritage language development. In *Heritage language development,* ed. S. Krashen, L. Tse, and J. McQuillan. Culver City, Calif.: Language Education Associates.

———. 1999. *Three arguments against whole language and why they are wrong.* Portsmouth, N.H.: Heinemann.

———. 2001. More smoke and mirrors: A critique of the National Reading Panel report on fluency. *Phi Delta Kappan* 83: 119–123.

———. 2002. The NRP comparison of whole language and phonics: Ignoring the crucial variable in reading. *Talking Points* 13(3): 22–28.

————. 2003a. *Explorations in language acquisition and use: The Taipei lectures.* Portsmouth, N.H.: Heinemann.

————. 2003b. The unbearable coolness of phonemic awareness. *Language Magazine* 2(8): 13–18.

————. 2003c. Three roles for reading. In *English learners: Reaching the highest level of English literacy,* ed. G. Garcia..International Reading Association.

————. 2003d. The (lack of) experimental evidence supporting the use of Accelerated Reader. *Journal of Children's Literature* 29 (2): 9, 16–30.

Krashen, S., and H. White. 1991. Is spelling acquired or learned? A re-analysis of Rice (1897) and Cornman (1902). *ITL: Review of Applied Linguistics* 91–92: 1–48.

Kyte, G. 1948. When spelling has been mastered in the elementary school. *Journal of Educational Research* 42: 47–53.

LaBrant, L. 1958. An evaluation of free reading. In *Research in the three R's,* ed. C. Hunnicutt and W. Iverson. New York: Harper, pp. 154–161.

Lai, F. K. 1993. The effect of a summer reading course on reading and writing skills. *System* 21(1): 87–100.

Lamme, L. 1976. Are reading habits and abilities related? *Reading Teacher* 30: 21–27.

Lancaster, T. 1928. A study of the voluntary reading of pupils in grdes IV-VIII. *Elementary School Journal* 28: 525–537.

Lance, K., C. Hamilton-Pennell, M. Rodney, L. Petersen, and C. Sitter, C. 1999. *Information empowered: The school librarian as an academic achievement in Alaska schools.* Juno: Alaska State Library.

Lance, K., M. Rodney, and C. Hamilton-Pennell. 2000a. *How school librarians help kids achieve standards: The second Colorado study.* San Jose: Hi Willow Research and Publishing.

————. 2000b. *Measuring to standards: The impact of school library programs and information literacy in Pennsylvania schools.* Greensburg, Pa.: Pennsylvania Citizens for Better Libraries (604 Hunt Club Drive, Greensburg PA, 15601).

————. 2001. *Good schools have school librarians: Oregon school librarians collaborate to improve academic achievement.* Salem: Oregon Educational Media Association.

Lance, K., L. Welborn, and C. Hamilton-Pennell. 1993.*The Impact of school library media centers on academic achievement.* Castle Rock, Colo.: Hi Willow Research and Publishing.

Langer, J., and A. Applebee. 1987. *How writing shapes thinking.* Urbana, Ill.: National Council of Teachers of English.

Langford, J., and Allen, E. 1983. The effects of U.S.S.R. on students' attitudes and achievements. *Reading Horizons* 23: 194–200.

Lao, C. Y. 2003. Prospective teachers' journey to becoming readers. *New Mexico Journal of Reading* 32(2): 14–20.

Lao, C. Y., and S. Krashen. 2000. The impact of popular literature study on literacy development in EFL: More evidence for the power of reading. *System* 28: 261–270.

Laufer, B. 2003. Vocabulary acquisition in a second language: Do learners really acquire most vocabulary by reading? Some empirical evidence. *The Canadian Modern Language Review* 59(4): 567–587.

Lawson, H. 1968. Effects of free reading on the reading achievement of sixth grade pupils. In *Forging ahead in reading,* ed. J. A. Figurel. Newark, Del: International Reading Association, pp. 501–504.

Lee, S. Y. 1998. Effects of introducing free reading and language acquisition theory on students' attitudes toward the English class. *Studies in English Language and Literature* 4: 21–28.

————. 2001. *What makes it difficult to write.* Taipei: Crane Publishing Company.

Lee, S. Y., and S. Krashen. 1996. Free voluntary reading and writing competence in Taiwanese high school students. *Perceptual and Motor Skills* 83: 687–690.

————. 1997. Writing apprehension in Chinese as a first language. *ITL: Review of Applied Linguistics* 115–116: 27–37.

Lee, S. Y., S. Krashen, and L. Tse. 1997. The author recognition test and vocabulary knowledge: A replication. *Perceptual and Motor Skills* 83: 648–650.

Lee, Y. O., S. Krashen, and B. Gribbons. 1996 The effect of reading on the acquisition of English relative clauses. *ITL: Review of Applied Linguistics* 113–114: 263–273.

LeMoine, N., B. Brandlin, B. O'Brian, and J. McQuillan. 1997. The (print)-rich get richer: Library access in low- and high-achieving elementary schools. *The California Reader* 30: 23–25.

Leonhardt, M. 1998. How to sweeten your school's climate for reading. *School Library Journal* 44(11): 28–31.

Leung, C., and J. Pikulski. 1990. Incidental learning of word meanings by kindergarten and first-grade children through repeated read aloud events. In *Literacy theory and research: Analysis from multiple paradigms*, ed. J. Zutell and S. McCormick. Chicago: National Reading Conference, pp. 281–301.

Liberman, M. 1979. The verbal language of television. *Journal of Reading* 26: 602–609.

Lituanas, P., G. Jacobs, and W. Renandya. 1999. A study of extensive reading with remedial reading students. In *Language instructional issues in Asian classrooms*, ed. Y. M. Cheah and S. M. Ng. Newark, N.J.: International Reading Association, pp. 89–104.

Lokke, V., and G. Wykoff. 1948. "Double writing" in freshman composition —an experiment. *School and Society* 68: 437–439.

Lomax, C. 1976. Interest in books and stories at nursery school. *Educational Research* 19: 110–112.

Lorge, I., and J. Chall. 1963. Estimating the size of vocabularies of children and adults: An analysis of methodological issues. *Journal of Experimental Education* 32: 147–157.

Lowrey, L., and W. Grafft. 1965. Paperback books and reading attitudes. *Reading Teacher* 21: 618–623.

Lyness, P. 1952. The place of the mass media in the lives of boys and girls. *Journalism Quarterly* 29: 43–54.

Maccoby, E. 1951. Television: Its impact on school children. *Public Opinion Quarterly* 15: 421–444.

MacDonald, H. 2003. Manga sales just keep rising. *Publishers Weekly*, March 17.

Manning, G., and M. Manning. 1984. What models of recreational reading make a difference? *Reading World* 23: 375–380.

Marshall, J. 1987. The effects of writing on students' understanding of literary texts. *Research in the Teaching of English* 21: 30–63.

Martinez, M., N. Roser, J. Worthy, S. Strecker, and P. Gough. 1997. Classroom libraries and children's book selections: Redefining "access" in self-selected reading. In *Inquires in literacy: Theory and practice. Forty-sixth yearbook of The National Reading Conference,* ed. C. Kinzer, K. Hinchman, and D. Leu. Chicago: National Reading Conference, pp. 265–272.

Mason, B. 2003. Evidence for the sufficiency of extensive reading on the development of grammatical accuracy. Doctoral dissertation, Temple University, Osaka, Japan.

Mason, B., and S. Krashen. 1997. Extensive reading in English as a foreign language. *System* 25: 91–102.

Mason, G., and W. Blanton. 1971. Story content for beginning reading instruction. *Elementary English* 48: 793–796.

Massimini, F., M. Csikszentmihalyi, and A. Della Fave. 1992. Flow and biocultural evolution. In *Optimal experience: Psychological studies of flow in consciousness,* ed. M. Csikszentmihalyi and I. Csikszentmihalyi. Cambridge: Cambridge University Press, pp. 60–81.

Mathabane, M. 1986. *Kaffir boy.* New York: Plume.

Mathis, D. 1996. *The effect of the Accelerated Reader program on reading comprehension.* ERIC Document No. ED 398 555.

Maynes, F. 1981. Uninterrupted sustained silent reading. *Reading Research Quarterly* 17: 159–160.

McCracken, R., and M. McCracken. 1978. Modeling is the key to sustained silent reading. *Reading Teacher* 31: 406–408.

McDonald, M., J. Harris, and J. Mann. 1966. Individual versus group instruction in first grade reading. *Reading Teacher* 19: 643–646, 652.

McEvoy, G., and C. Vincent. 1980. Who reads and why? *Journal of Communication* 30: 134–140.

McKenna, M., D. Kear, and R. Ellsworth. 1991. Developmental trends in children's use of print media: A national study. In *Learner factors/teacher factors: Issues in literacy research and instruction,* ed. J. Zutell and S. McCormick. Chicago: National Reading Conference, pp. 319–324.

McLoyd, V. 1979. The effects of extrinsic rewards of differential value on high and low intrinsic interest. *Child Development* 10: 1010–1019.

McQuillan, J. 1994. Reading versus grammar: What students think is pleasurable for language acquisition. *Applied Language Learning* 5: 95–100.

———. 1996. How should heritage languages be taught? The effects of a free voluntary reading program. *Foreign Language Annals* 29(1): 56–72.

———. 1997. The effects of incentives on reading. *Reading Research and Instruction* 36: 111–125.

———. 1998a. *The literacy crisis: False claims and real solutions.* Portsmouth, N.H.: Heinemann.

———. 1998b. The use of self-selected and free voluntary reading in heritage language programs: A review of research. In *Heritage language development,* ed. S. Krashen, L. Tse, and J. McQuillan. Culver City, Calif.: Language Education Associates, pp. 73–87.

McQuillan, J., and J. Au. 2001. The effect of print access on reading frequency. *Reading Psychology* 22: 225–248.

McQuillan, J., and V. Rodrigo. 1998. Literature-based programs for first language development: Giving native bilinguals access to books. In *Literacy, Access, and Libraries Among the Language Minority Population,* ed. R. Constantino. Lanham, Md.: Scarecrow, pp. 209–224.

Medrich, E., A. Roizen, V. Rubin, and S. Buckley. 1982. *The serious business of growing up: A study of children's lives outside school.* Los Angeles: University of California Press.

Mellon, C. 1987. Teenagers do read: What rural youth say about leisure reading. *School Library Journal* 38(8): 27–30.

Miller, F. 1986. *The Dark Knight returns.* New York: DC Comics.

Miller, G. 1977. *Spontaneous apprentices: Children and language.* New York: Seabury.

Miller, M., and M. Shontz. 2001. New money, old books. *School Library Journal* 47(10): 5–60.

Minton, M. 1980. The effect of sustained silent reading upon comprehension and attitudes among ninth graders. *Journal of Reading* 23: 498–502.

Monteith, M. 1980. How well does the average American read? Some facts, figures and opinions. *Journal of Reading* 20: 460–464.

Moore, A. 1986. *Watchmen.* New York: DC Comics.

Morrow, L. 1982. Relationships between literature programs, library corner designs, and children's use of literature. *Journal of Educational Research* 75: 339–344.

———. 1983. Home and school correlates of early interest in literature. *Journal of Educational Research* 75: 339–344.

Morrow, L., and C. Weinstein. 1982. Increasing children's use of literature through program and physical changes. *Elementary School Journal* 83: 131–137.

Munoz, H. 2003. First Lady delivers $5,000 and a passion for reading. *Education Week,* May 21.

Murray, J., and S. Kippax. 1978. Children's social behavior in three towns with differing television experience. *Reading Teacher* 28: 19–29.

Nagy, W., R. Anderson, and P. Herman. 1987. Learning word meanings from context during normal reading. *American Educational Research Journal* 24: 237–270.

Nagy, W., and P. Herman. 1987. Breadth and depth of vocabulary knowledge: Implications for acquisition and instruction. In *The nature of vocabulary acquisition,* ed. M. McKeown and M. Curtiss. Hillsdale, N.J.: Erbaum, pp. 19–35.

Nagy, W., P. Herman, and R. Anderson. 1985. Learning words from context. *Reading Research Quarterly* 23: 6–50.

National Council on Writing. 2003. *The neglected "R": The need for a writing revolution.* New York: College Entrance Examination Board.

National Institute of Child Health and Human Development (NICHD). 2000. *Report of the National Reading Panel. Teaching children to read.* [NIH Publication no. 00-4754]. Washington, DC: Government Printing Office.

NCES, 2000. *A study of the differences between higher- and lower-performing Indiana schools in reading and mathematics.* Oak Brook, Ill.: North Central Regional Educational Laboratory.

Nell, V. 1988. *Lost in a book.* New Haven, Conn.: Yale University Press.

Neuman, S. 1986. The home environment and fifth-grade students' leisure reading. *Elementary School Journal* 86: 335–343.

———. 1988. The displacement effect: Assessing the relation between television viewing and reading performance. *Reading Research Quarterly* 23: 414–440.

———. 1995. *Literacy in the television age: The myth of the TV effect.* 2d ed. Norwood, N.J.: Ablex.

Neuman, S., and D. Celano. 2001. Access to print in low-income and middle-income communities. *Reading Research Quarterly* 36(1): 8–26.

Newell, G. 1984. Learning while writing in two content areas: A case study/protocol analysis. *Research in the Teaching of English* 18: 265–287.

Newell, G., and P. Winograd. 1989. The effects of writing on learning from expository text. *Written Communication* 6: 196–217.

Nisbet, S. 1941. The scientific investigation of spelling instruction: Two preliminary investigations. *British Journal of Educational Psychology* 11: 150.

Norton, B. 2003. The motivating power of comic books: Insights from Archie comic book readers. *The Reading Teacher* 57(2): 140–147.

O'Brian, I. 1931. A comparison of the use of intensive training and wide reading in the improvement of reading. *Educational Method* 10: 346–349.

Oliver, M. 1973. The effect of high intensity practice on reading comprehension. *Reading Improvement* 10: 16–18.

———. 1976. The effect of high intensity practice on reading achievement. *Reading Improvement* 13: 226–228.

Oller, D. K, and R. Eilers. 2002. *Language and literacy in bilingual children.* Clevedon, England: Multilingual Matters.

Ormrod, J. 1986. Learning to spell while reading: A follow-up study. *Perceptual and Motor Skills* 63: 652–654.

Pack, S. 2000. Public library use, school performance, and the parental X-factor: A bio-documentary approach to children's snapshots. *Reading Improvement* 37: 161–172.

Parrish, B. 1983. Put a little romance into your reading program. *Journal of Reading* 26: 610–615.

Parrish, B., and K. Atwood. 1985. Enticing readers: The teen romance craze. *California Reader* 18: 22–27.

Pavonetti, L., K. Brimmer, and J. Cipielewski, J. 2003. Accelerated reader: What are the lasting effects on the reading habits of middle school students exposed to Accelerated Reader in elementary grades? *Journal of Adolescent and Adult Literacy* 46(4): 300–311.

Petre, B. 1971. Reading breaks make it in Maryland. *The Reading Teacher* 15: 191–194.

Pfau, D. 1967. Effects of planned recreational reading programs. *Reading Teacher* 21: 34–39.

Pilgreen, J. 2000. *The SSR handbook: How to organize and maintain a sustained silent reading program.* Portsmouth, N.H.: Heinemann.

Pilgreen, J., and S. Krashen. 1993. Sustained silent reading with high school ESL students: Impact on reading comprehension, reading frequency, and reading enjoyment. *School Library Media Quarterly* 22: 21–23.

Pitts, M., H. White, and S. Krashen. 1989. Acquiring second language vocabulary through reading: A replication of the Clockwork Orange study using second language acquirers. *Reading in a Foreign Language* 5: 271–275.

Pitts, S. 1986. Read aloud to adult learners? Of course! *Reading Psychology* 7: 35–42.

Polak, J., and S. Krashen. 1988. Do we need to teach spelling? The relationship between spelling and voluntary reading among community college ESL students. *TESOL Quarterly* 22: 141–146.

Postman, N. 1983. The disappearing child. *Educational Leadership* 40: 10–17.

Postlethwaite, T., and K. N. Ross. 1992. *Effective schools in reading: Implications for educational planners. An exploratory study.* The Hague: The International Association for the Evaluation of Educational Achievement.

Potter, W. 1987. Does television viewing hinder academic achievement among adolescents? *Human Communications Research* 14: 27–46.

Pucci, S. 1994. Supporting Spanish language literacy: Latino children and free reading resources in the schools. *Bilingual Research Journal* 18: 67–82.

Pucci, S., and S. Ulanoff. 1996. Where are the books? *The CATESOL Journal* 9(2): 111–116.

Pulido, D. 2003. Modeling the role of second language proficiency and topic familiarity in second language incidental vocabulary acquisition through reading. *Language Learning* 53(2): 233–284.

Ramirez, D., S. Yuen, D. Ramey, and D. Pasta. 1991. *Final report: Longitudinal study of structured English immersion strategy, early-exit and late-exit bilingual education programs for language minority students, Vol. I.* San Mateo, Calif.: Aguirre International.

Ramos, F., and S. Krashen. 1998. The impact of one trip to the public library: Making books available may be the best incentive for reading. *The Reading Teacher* 51(7): 614–615.

Ravitch, D., and C. Finn. 1987. *What do our 17–year-olds know?* New York: Harper & Row.

Reed, C. 1985. *Reading adolescents: The young adult book and the school.* New York: Holt Rinehart Winston.

Rehder, L. 1980. Reading skills in a paperback classroom. *Reading Horizons* 21: 16–21.

Renaissance Reader, Report 36: Maine middle school achieves academic success with Renaissance comprehensive schoolwide program. Available: www.renlearn. com.

Renandya, W., B. R. S. Rajan, and G. Jacobs. 1999. ER with adult learns of English as a second language. *RELC Journal* 30(1): 39–61.

Reutzel, R., and P. Hollingsworth. 1991. Reading comprehension skills: Testing the distinctiveness hypothesis. *Reading Research and Instruction* 30: 32–46.

Rice, E. 1986. The everyday activities of adults: Implications for prose recall —Part I. *Educational Gerontology* 12: 173–186.

Rice, J. 1897. The futility of the spelling grind. *Forum* 23: 163–172, 409–419.

Rice, M., and P. Haight. 1986. "Motherese" of Mr. Rogers: A description of the dialogue of educational television programs. *Journal of Speech and Hearing Disorders* 51: 282–287.

Richard, A. 2003. GAO says costs for state tests all in how questions asked. *Education Week,* May 21.

Richards, A. 1920. Spelling and the individual system. *School and Society* 10: 647–650.

Roberts, D., C. Bachen, M. Hornby, and P. Hernandez-Ramos. 1984. Reading and television: Predictors of reading achievement at different age levels. *Communication Research* 11(1): 9–49.

Robinson, J. 1972. Television's impact on everyday life: Some cross-national evidence. In *Television and social behavior, vol. 4,* ed. E. Rubinstein, G. Comstock, and J. Murray. Rockwell, Md.: National Institute of Mental Health, pp. 410–431.

———. 1980. The changing reading habits of the American public. *Journal of Communication* 30: 141–152.

Robinson, J., and G. Godbey. 1997. *Time for life: The surprising way Americans use their time.* University Park: University of Pennsylvania Press.

Rodney, M., K. Lance, and C. Hamilton-Pennell, 2002. *Make the connection: Quality school library media programs impact academic achievement in Iowa.* Bettendorf, Iowa: Mississippi Bend Area Educational Agency.

Rodrigo, V. 1997. Son concientes los estudiantes de Espagnol intermedio de los beneficios que les brinda la lectura? *Hispania* 80: 255–264.

Rodrigo, V., J. McQuillan, and S. Krashen. 1996. Free voluntary reading and vocabulary knowledge in native speakers of Spanish. *Perceptual and Motor Skills* 83: 648–650.

Rosenthal, N. 1995. *Speaking of reading.* Portsmouth, N.H.: Heinemann.

Ross, P. 1978. Getting books into those empty hands. *Reading Teacher* 31: 397–399.

Rucker, B. 1982. Magazines and teenage reading skills: Two controlled field experiments. *Journalism Quarterly* 59: 28–33.

Sadowski, M. 1980. An attitude survey for sustained silent reading programs. *Journal of Reading* 23: 721–726.

Salyer, M. 1987. A comparison of the learning characteristics of good and poor ESL writers. *Applied Linguistics Interest Section Newsletter, TESOL* 8: 2–3.

San Diego County. 1965. A plan for research. In *Individualized reading: Readings*, ed. S. Duker. Metuchen, N.J.: Scarecrow, pp. 359–363.

Saragi, Y., P. Nation, and G. Meister. 1978. Vocabulary learning and reading. *System* 6: 70–78.

Sartain, H. 1960. The Roseville experiment with individualized reading. *Reading Teacher* 12: 277–281.

Sato, I. 1992. Bosozuku: Flow in Japanese motorcycle gangs. In *Optimal experience: Psychological studies of flow in consciousness.* ed. M. Csikszentmihalyi and I. Csikszentmihalyi. Cambridge: Cambridge University Press, pp. 92–117.

Schafer, C., and A. Anastasi. 1968. A biographical inventory for identifying creativity in adolescent boys. *Journal of Applied Psychology* 58: 42–48.

Schatz, E., and R. Baldwin. 1986. Context clues are unreliable predictors of word meanings. *Reading Research Quarterly* 20: 439–453.

Schon, I., K. Hopkins, and C. Vojir. 1984. The effects of Spanish reading emphasis on the English and Spanish reading abilities of Hispanic high school students. *Bilingual Review* 11: 33–39.

———. 1985. The effects of special reading time in Spanish on the reading abilities and attitudes of Hispanic junior high school students. *Journal of Psycholinguistic Research* 14: 57–65.

Schoolboys of Barbiana. 1970. *Letter to a teacher.* New York: Vintage Books.

Schoonover, R. 1938. The case for voluminous reading. *English Journal* 27: 114–118

Schramm, W., J. Lyle, and E. Parker. 1961. *Television in the lives of our children.* Stanford, Calif.: Stanford University Press.

Seashore, R., and L. Eckerson. 1940. The measurement of individual differences in general English vocabularies. *Journal of Educational Psychology* 31: 14–31.

Segal, J. 1997. Summer daze. Class paper, Trenton State University, Summer.

Senechal, M., J. LeFebre, E. Hudson, and E. Lawson. 1996. Knowledge of storybooks as a predictor of young children's vocabulary. *Journal of Educational Psychology* 88(1): 520–536.

Shanahan, T. 2000. Reading Panel: A member responds to a critic. *Education Week*, May 31, 39.

Shin, F. 1998. Implementing free voluntary reading with ESL middle school students—improvement in attitudes toward reading and test scores. In *Literacy, access, and libraries among the language minority population*, ed. R. Constantino. Lanham, Md.: Scarecrow, pp. 225–234.

———. 2001. Motivating students with Goosebumps and other popular books. *CSLA Journal (California School Library Association)* 25(1): 15–19.

———. 2003. Should we just tell them to read? The role of direct encouragement in promoting recreational reading. *Knowledge Quest* 32(3): 49–50.

Shooter, J. 1986. Marvel and me. In *The comic book price guide*, ed. R. Overstreet. New York: Harmony Books, pp. A85–96.

Simonton, D. 1984. *Genius, creativity, and leadership.* Cambridge, Mass.: Harvard University Press.

———. 1988. Scientific genius: A psychology of science. Cambridge, Mass.: Harvard University Press.

Slover, V. 1959. Comic books vs. story books. *Elementary English* 36: 319–322.

SmartGirl Internette, Inc. 1999. *Teen Read Week Report,* November.

Smith, C., R. Constantino, and S. Krashen. 1996. Differences in print environment for children in Beverly Hills, Compton and Watts. *Emergency Librarian* 24(4): 4–5.

Smith, E. 2001. *Texas school libraries: Standards, resources, services and students' performance.* Austin: Texas State Libraries and Archives Commission.

Smith, F. 1988. *Joining the literacy club.* Portsmouth, N.H.: Heinemann.

———. 1994a. *Writing and the writer.* 2d ed. Hillsdale, N.J.: Erlbaum.

———. 1994b. *Understanding reading.* 5th ed. Hillsdale, N.J.: Erlbaum.

Smith, M. 1941. Measurement of the size of general English vocabulary through the elementary grades and high school. *Genetic Psychology Monographs* 24: 311–345.

Smith, R., and G. Supanich. 1984. *The vocabulary scores of company presidents.* Chicago: Johnson O'Conner Research Foundation Technical Report 1984–1.

Snow, C., W. Barnes, J. Chandler, I. Goodman, and H. Hemphill. 1991. *Unfulfilled expectations: Home and school influences on literacy.* Cambridge, Mass.: Harvard University Press.

Sommers, N. 1980. Revision strategies of student writers and experienced adult writers. *College Composition and Communication* 31: 378–388.

Southgate, V., H. Arnold, and S. Johnson. 1981. *Extending beginning reading.* London: Heinemann Educational Books.

Sperzl, E. 1948. The effect of comic books on vocabulary growth and reading comprehension. *Elementary English* 25: 109–113.

Stahl, S., M. Richek., and R. Vandevier. 1991. Learning meaning vocabulary through listening: A sixth-grade replication. In *Learner factors/teacher factors: Issues in literacy research and instruction,* ed. J. Zutell and S. McCormick. Chicago: National Reading Conference, pp. 185–192.

Stanovich, K., and A. Cunningham. 1992. Studying the consequences of literacy within a literate society: the cognitive correlates of print exposure. *Memory and Cognition* 20(1): 51–68.

———. 1993. Where does knowledge come from? Specific associations between print exposure and information acquisition. *Journal of Educational Psychology* 85(2): 211–229.

Stanovich, K., and R. West. 1989. Exposure to print and orthographic processing. *Reading Research Quarterly* 24: 402–433.

Stanovich, K., R. West, and M. Harrison. 1995. Knowledge growth and maintenance across the life span: The role of print exposure. *Developmental Psychology* 31(5): 811–826.

Stedman, L., and C. Kaestle. 1987. Literacy and reading performance in the United States, from 1880 to the present. *Reading Research Quarterly* 22: 59–78.

Stokes, J., S. Krashen, and J. Kartchner. 1998. Factors in the acquisition of the present subjunctive in Spanish: The role of reading and study. *ITL: Review of Applied Linguistics* 121–122: 19–25.

Summers, E., and J. V. McClelland. 1982. A field-based evaluation of sustained silent reading (SSR) in intermediate grades. *Alberta Journal of Educational Research* 28: 110–112.

Sutton, R. 1985. Librarians and the paperback romance. *School Library Journal* 32: 253–258.

Swain, E. 1948. Using comic books to teach reading and language arts. *Journal of Reading* 22: 253–258.

Swanborn, M., and K. de Glopper. 1999. Incidental word learning while reading: A meta-analysis. *Review of Educational Research* 69(3): 261–285.

Swanton, S. 1984. Minds alive: What and why gifted students read for pleasure. *School Library Journal* 30: 99–102.

Thompson, M. 1956. Why not try self-selection? *Elementary English* 33: 486–490.

Thompson, R. 1930. *The effectiveness of modern spelling instruction.* New York: Columbia University Teacher's College. Contributions to Education, No. 436.

Thorndike, R. 1941. Words and the comics. *Journal of Experimental Education* 10: 110–113.

———. 1973. *Reading comprehension education in fifteen countries.* New York: Halsted Press.

Trelease, J. 2001. *The read-aloud handbook.* 5th ed. New York: Penguin.

Tsang, W-K., 1996. Comparing the effects of reading and writing on writing performance. *Applied Linguistics* 17(2): 210–233.

Tse, L. 1996. When an ESL adult becomes a reader. *Reading Horizons* 31(1): 16–29.

———. 1998. Ethnic identity formation and its implications for heritage language development. In *Heritage language development.* ed. S. Krashen, L. Tse, and J. McQuillan. Culver City, Calif.: Language Education Associates, pp. 15–29.

———. 2001. Resisting and reversing language shift: Heritage-language resilience among U.S. native biliterates. *Harvard Educational Review* 71(4): 676–706.

Tudor, I., and F. Hafiz. 1989. Extensive reading as a means of input to L2 learning. *Journal of Research in Reading* 12(2): 164–178.

Twadell, F. 1973. Vocabulary expansion in the TESOL classroom. *TESOL Quarterly* 7: 61–78.

Ujiie, J., and S. Krashen.. 1996a. Comic book reading, reading enjoyment, and pleasure reading among middle class and chapter I middle school students. *Reading Improvement* 33 (1): 51–54.

———. 1996b. Is comic book reading harmful? Comic book reading, school achievement, and pleasure reading among seventh graders. *California School Library Association Journal* 19(2): 27–28.

———. 2002. Home run books and reading enjoyment. *Knowledge Quest* 3(1): 36–37.

Van Zelst, R., and W. Kerr. 1951. Some correlates of technical and scientific productivity. *Journal of Abnormal Psychology* 46: 470–475.

Varble, M. 1990. Analysis of writing samples of students taught by teachers using whole language and traditional approaches. *Journal of Educational Research* 83: 245–251.

Vollands, S., K. Topping, and R. Evans. 1996. *Experimental evaluation of computer assisted self-assessment of reading comprehension: Effects on reading achievement and attitude.* ERIC Document ED 408 567.

———. 1999. Computerized self-assessment of reading comprehension with the accelerated reader: Action research. *Reading and Writing Quarterly* 15: 197–211.

Von Sprecken, D., and S. Krashen. 1998. Do students read during sustained silent reading? *California Reader* 32(1): 11–13.

———. 2002. Is there a decline in the reading romance? *Knowledge Quest* 30(3): 11–17.

Von Sprecken, D., J. Kim, and S. Krashen. 2000. The home run book: Can one positive reading experience create a reader? *California School Library Journal* 23(2): 8–9.

Walker, G., and I. Kuerbitz. 1979. Reading to preschoolers as an aid to successful beginning reading. *Reading Improvement* 16: 149–154.

Wallas, G. 1926. *The art of thought. London: C.A. Watts.* (Abridged version, 1945). Excerpts reprinted in *Creativity,* ed. P. E. Vernon (1970). Middlesex, England: Penguin, pp. 91–97.

Waring, R., and M. Takakei. 2003. At what rate do learners learn and retain new vocabulary from reading a graded reader? *Reading in a Foreign Language* 15(2): 130–163.

Wayne, R. 1954. Survey of interest in comic books. *School Activities* 25: 244.

Weiner, S. 2003. Mutants for the masses: Graphic novel roundup. *School Library Journal* 49 (5): 32–33.

Wells, G. 1985. *Language development in the pre-school years.* Cambridge: Cambridge University Press.

Wendelin, K., and R. Zinck. 1983. How students make book choices. *Reading Horizons* 23: 84–88.

Wertham, F. 1954. *Seduction of the innocent.* New York: Rinehart.

Wesche, M. and T.S. Paribakht 1996. Assessing second language vocabulary knowledge: Depth versus breadth. *Canadian Modern Language Review* 53(1): 13–40.

West, R., and K. Stanovich. 1991. The incidental acquisition of information from reading. *Psychological Science* 2: 325–330.

West, R., K. Stanovich, and H. Mitchell. 1993. Reading in the real world and its correlates. *Reading Research Quarterly* 28: 35–50.

Wheldall, K., and J. Entwhistle. 1988. Back in the USSR: The effect of teacher modeling of silent reading on pupils' reading behaviour in the primary school classroom. *Educational Psychology* 8: 51–56.

White, T., M. Graves, and W. Slater. 1990. Growth of reading vocabulary in diverse elementary schools: Decoding and word meaning. *Journal of Educational Psychology* 82: 281–290.

Wilde, S. 1990. A proposal for a new spelling curriculum. *Elementary School Journal* 90: 275–290.

Williams, P., and M. Boyes. 1986. Television-viewing patterns and use of other media. In *The impact of television,* ed. T. M. Williams. New York: Academic Press, pp. 215–263.

Williams, P., E. Haertel, G. Haertel, and H. Walberg. 1982. The impact of leisure-time television on school learning: A research synthesis. *American Educational Research Journal* 19: 19–50.

Willig, A. 1985. A meta-analysis of selected studies on the effectiveness of bilingual education. *Review of Educational Research* 55(3): 269–317.

Willingham, D. 2002. Allocating student study time: "Massed" versus "distributed" practice. *American Educator* (Summer). Available: http://www.aft.org/american_educator/summer2002/askcognitivescientist.html.

Witty, P. 1941. Reading the comics: A comparative study. *Journal of Experimental Education* 10: 105–109.

Witty, P., and R. Sizemore. 1954. Reading the comics: A summary of studies and an evaluation, I. Elementary English 31: 501–506.

———. 1955. Reading the comics: A summary of studies and an evaluation, III. *Elementary English* 32: 109–114.

Wolf, A., and L. Mikulecky. 1978. Effects of uninterrupted sustained silent reading and of reading skills instruction on changes in secondary school students' reading attitudes and achievement. In *27th Yearbook of the National Reading Conference.* Clemson, S.C.: National Reading Conference, pp. 226–228.

Worthy, J. 1998. "On every page someone gets killed!" Book conversations you don't hear in school. *Journal of Adolescent and Adult Literacy* 41(7): 508–517.

———. 2000. Teachers' and students' suggestions for motivating middle-school children to read. In *49th yearbook of the National Reading Conference,* ed. T. Shanahan, and F. Rodriguez-Brown. Chicago: National Reading Conference, pp. 441–451.

Worthy, J., and S. McKool. 1996. Students who say they hate to read: The importance of opportunity, choice, and access. In *Literacies for the 21st century: Research and practice,* ed. D. Leu, C. Kinzer, and K. Hinchman. Chicago: National Reading Conference, pp. 245–256.

Worthy, J., M. Moorman, and M. Turner. 1999. What Johnny likes to read is hard to find in school. *Reading Research Quarterly* 34(10): 12–27.

Wright, G. 1979. The comic book: A forgotten medium in the classroom. *Reading Teacher* 33: 158–161.

Wright, R. 1966. *Black boy.* New York: Harper & Row.

Yoon, J-C. 2002. Three decades of sustained silent reading: A meta-analytic review of the effects of SSR on attitude toward reading. *Reading Improvement* 39(4): 186–195.

Zuckerman, D., D. Singer, and J. Singer. 1980. Television viewing, children's reading, and related classroom behavior. *Journal of Communication* 32: 166–174.

Researcher Index

Subject Index

About the Author

STEPHEN D. KRASHEN is Emeritus Professor of Education at the University of Southern California. He is best known for his work in establishing a general theory of second language acquisition, as the cofounder of the Natural Approach, and as the inventor of sheltered subject matter teaching. He is the author of numerous books.